PARISIENNE FRENCH

Chic Phrases, Slang & Style

Rhianna Jones

Ulysses Press

Published by
Ulysses Press
P.O. Box 3440
Berkeley, CA 94703
www.ulyssespress.com

ISBN: 978-1-61243-227-4
Library of Congress Catalog Number 2013938625

Printed in the United States by Bang Printing

10 9 8 7 6 5 4 3 2 1

Acquisitions editor: Keith Riegert
Project editor: Alice Riegert
French editor: Vincent Vichit-Vadakan
English editor: Lauren Harrison
Proofreader: Elyce Berrigan-Dunlop
Front cover design: Jenna Stempel
Interior design and chapter icons: Rebecca Lown
Illustrator: Tatiana Minina

Distributed by Publishers Group West

Anikó,

I dedicate this book to you, *chérie*, the best friend a girl could ever wish for. With your beauty, strength, and overall *élan*, you are the quintessential *Parisienne*. I can only hope that these chapters inspire my readers in the way you continue to inspire me.

Mille tendresse,

Rhianna

Table of Contents

Introduction: L'Introduction

"Paris is the city in which one loves to live."

—MARGARET ANDERSON

You're the girl who's got it all: personality, ambition, intelligence, and killer style. And guess what? You're about to take your fabulous self to Paris. Perhaps you've been dreaming about it your whole life, or maybe it's simply one of the many escapades on your radar. The point is: the standard travel guide isn't gonna cut it for you; you need something to match your level of *je ne sais quoi*. That something, my dear, is *Parisienne French*.

In essence, this book introduces you to the current slang, culture, and lifestyle you'll encounter during your Parisian exploits. As this is not an in-depth grammar guide, it is best for someone who has a basic understanding of the French language. The vocabulary here is mainly stuff you'll wanna say around your cool new friends or some hot Parisian piece at a bar; it's not professionally minded. Picture this: if you find yourself about to blow your weekly allowance on a vital pair of heels and wanna tell your Parisian BFF *en français*, now you can. Or, when your new crush asks you to pick a place to meet up, which *arrondisement* should you choose? We've got you covered.

That being said, even if French is completely foreign to you, you're a smart cookie, and with the included pronunciation tools and explanatory notes here, you'll figure it out. Promise. Also note that this is not a travel guide. Rather than telling you what to see or do, the chapters paint a portrait of the city's vibes so that you can discover it yourself. The more personal your experience is, the fonder your memories will be. Parks, benches, and cafés are scattered all over the city, so take a seat and watch the day go by. Think of Paris as an incredibly stylish circus and study the spectacle in front of you. This book notes the cultural differences in dress, speech, etiquette, etc.; look around and see them play out. Incorporate all that loveliness into your natural way of being and—*voilà!*—you've become a more *parisienne* you. *Parisienne French* will keep you cultured, chic, and most importantly, communicating. Cue the literary love affair.

Trust me, Paris *is* all it's cracked up to be, and then some. With an open mind, a charming smile, and this book, you'll have the city in the palm of your hand pronto. *La vie parisienne* is just a few chapters away ...

Chapter 1

Essentials: Les Essentiels

"If you want to establish an international presence, you can't do so
from New York. You need the consecration of Paris."

—OSCAR DE LA RENTA

Something about the French language and culture has an internationally recognized aura of chic. A tongue whose words roll off melodically, yet seem so difficult to grasp to the foreign ear, *le français* makes the heart sing. It is often deemed the most beautiful language in the world, and perhaps its *cachet* lies in its gorgeous complexity. In fact, there are rules that exist in French simply based on aesthetics and the euphony of words. The countless vowels, gender/number agreements, and formality conventions are just a small part of what makes the language so *particulier*. This is not, however, meant to be discouraging in the least. It will take a bit of time and a lot of patience, but the more you challenge yourself to speak the language, the faster you'll pick it up. Even if you think you sound silly, finishing your convo with a smile will make your efforts all the more appreciated. Practice makes perfect, darling, and mastering *le français* will be the cherry on top of your cosmopolitan sundae.

Pronunciation
LA PRONONCIATION

One of the many charms French people have is their pride. Call it arrogance, call it pretension, but they've got a fine culture and they're damn proud of it. Considering how they've essentially seduced the entire world with their mother tongue, it's only natural they *love* their language. Like, a lot. Parisians hold their accent in higher esteem than that of the rest of the country, and a bit of a rivalry exists between urban Paris and rural France.

That being said, Parisians don't particularly appreciate hearing their language butchered, so don't be surprised if in some of your attempts to *parler* (to talk), you are responded to in English. You're trying to embrace the culture, they're trying to make your struggle easier, *c'est la vie*. It's not simply about getting the words out and in the right order, but more the fluidity and melody of what you're saying. They speak softer and as such their mouths are much tighter in speech than ours. Listen to those around you and pay close attention to how they sound. The more you remember that, the more likely you'll catch yourself mispronouncing something. Regardless, here's a lil' guide to get your parleying up to *parisienne* standards.

LETTER	PRONUNCIATION	EXAMPLE
a, à	ah	***Chanel**, shah-nel*
b	buh	***bordel**, bordehll (hot mess)*
c+a, o, u	kah	***café**, kah-fay (coffee)*
c+e, i,	say	***cinéma**, sin-ay-ma (movies)*
ç	say	***garçon**, gawr-sohn (boy)*
ch	sh	***cher**, shair (dear/expensive)*
d	duh	***jeudi**, zhuh-dee (Thursday)*
e	eh	***merci**, mehr-see (thank you)*
è	eh	***mère**, mehr (mother)*
é	ay	***marché**, mar-shay (market)*
-er, -ez, ai	ay	***j'ai**, zhay (I have); **donner**, dohn-ay (to give)*
eu (as part of a word)	uh	***dégueulasse**, day-guhl-lass (disgusting)*
eu (as a stand-alone word)	ooh (rhymes with "tu")	***j'ai eu**, zhay ooh (I had)*
f	fuh	***faire**, fair (to do)*
g+a, o, u	hard g (like "go")	***grand**, grawn (big)*
g+e, i	zh (like French "j," like the "s" in pleasure)	***nager**, nah-zhay (to swim)*
h	always silent	***homme**, ohm (man)*
i	ee	***amitié**, aw-mee-tee-ay (friendship)*
j	zh (like the "s" in pleasure)	***jeunesse**, zhuh-ness (youth)*
k	kuh	***kiffer**, kee-fay (to like)*
l	luh	***lettre**, leht-reh (letter)*
m	muh	***mode**, mohde (fashion)*

1

✂

LETTER	PRONUNCIATION	EXAMPLE
n	nuh	*nouveau*, *nooh-voh* (new)
o, ô	oh	*hôtel*, *ohtel* (hotel)
oi	wah	*moi*, *mwah* (me)
ou	ooh	*toujours*, *tooh-joor* (everyday/always)
p	puh	*peau*, *poh* (skin)
q	like the English "k"	*maquillage*, *mah-key-ahge* (makeup)
r	ruh	*restaurant*, *rest-oh-rawn* (restaurant)
s	suh	*bonsoir*, *bone-swahr* (good night); *visite*, *vee-zeet* (visit)
t	taw	*table*, *taw-bleh* (table)
t+ion	see-on	*nation*, *nah-see-on* (nation)
u	ooh	*rue*, *rooh* (street)
v	veh	*venir*, *veh-near* (to come)
w	veh	*WC*, *vay-say* (water closet)
x	eeks	*s'exciter*, *sex-see-tay* (to arouse)
y	yuh and ee	*yeux*, *yuh* (eyes); *stylé*, *stee-lay* (stylish)
z	zeh	*zéro*, *zay-roh* (zero)

Note: Many subtle nuances exist in French pronunciation that are difficult to articulate in text, specifically the "r," whether or not to pronounce the consonant at the end of a word, and common nasal sounds like *en* and *un*. The best way to master it is by listening closely to the natives around you.

If there is a final "e" after a consonant, you'll usually pronounce the consonant. Say *petit* (peh-tee), but *petite* (peh-teet).

In proper spoken French, sounding the final consonant happens even if the vowel that follows it is in the next word. In casual speech this happens less these days, but in many expressions it's indispensable. So *c'est ici* (it's here) is pronounced "set ee-see" vs. *c'est là-bas* (it's over there) "say la bah."

The French "r" is the one often depicted comically as if you're choking. It's not that harsh, but it's the opposite of the Spanish rolled "r." With French you act as if you were pronouncing the entire "r" sound but you hold back and continue to the next letter. Imagine pronouncing gargle, while gargling, that's where the French "r" comes from and how it sounds. You try to make it out, but can't quite finish. It's all in the back of the throat.

Grammar LA GRAMMAIRE

Le français is as complex as it is chic and as demanding as it is delightful. Mastering any language is an arduous process, and this one tends to be particularly difficult. Regardless, it's worth the effort; having French roll out of your adorable mouth ups your sex/sophistication appeal like no other, babe. This is also because it's a romance language, i.e., it derived from Latin way back when and is similar-ish to

Spanish, Portuguese, Italian, and Romanian. If you've got any of these down, it'll come more naturally. The French like sticking to their old-school roots, and some of the verbosity might seem a bit unnecessary to an anglophone. So while it might take them three words—*avoir besoin de* (have the need for)—to say what we would with four letters—"need"—it's a rather literal language and that's just the way it goes. Patience is a virtue, and the more patient you are with yourself the more fabulous you'll feel as you get your French on. Now go on girl, don't be shy …

Note: These are general rules. There are always exceptions to the rules and in French there are twice as many. Consult a grammar guide for the particulars. Likewise, verb conjugation is *very* complicated, so you'll def need a separate book for that if you want a deeper understanding.

Gender/Number/Agreement

Every noun in French has a gender (masculine/feminine) and is either singular or plural. The articles they take are also gender specific. For example:

Indefinite article "a/an/some":

> *un ami* (a friend, m.)
> *une amie* (a friend, f.)
> *des amis* (some friends, mpl.)
> *des amies* (some friends, fpl.)

Definite article "the":

le client (the customer, m.)
la cliente (the customer, f.)
les clients (the customers, mpl.)
les clientes (the customers, fpl.)

The definite articles are: *le* (ms), *la* (fs), and *les* (m/fpl). But in the case that the noun begins with a vowel or an unaspirated "h," the article changes to *l'*. For example: *l'étudiant* ("the student" m.) / *l'étudiante* ("the student" f.)

The plural stays the same because *les* ends in "s." For example: *les étudiants* (mpl.) / *les étudiantes* (fpl.)

An "s" added to the end of most nouns will make it plural. For nouns that already end in "s" you simply change the article.

In a group of people, any male presence signifies a masculine pronoun. Even if there is one boy and twenty girls, you use the masculine plural pronoun.

Any adjective that modifies a noun must agree with its gender/number. For example:

le joli garçon (the pretty boy)
la jolie fille (a pretty girl)
les jolis garçons (the pretty boys)
les jolies filles (the pretty girls)

Same as with nouns, adding an "e" to the adjective makes it feminine, and an "s" plural. So for the feminine plural form, an "es" would be added.

Adjective/Adverb Placement

In general, French adjectives come after the noun. For example: *le pull gris* (the gray sweater)

However, the commonly used BANGS adjectives (Beauty, Age, Number, Goodness, and Size) precede nouns. Some have irregular masculine/feminine forms:

Beauty: *beau/belle* (beautiful), *joli/jolie* (pretty)

> *Regarde tes **belles** jambes dans ta nouvelle robe noire!*
> Look at your **beautiful** legs in your new black dress!

Age: *jeune* (young), *vieux/vielle* (old), *nouveau/nouvelle* (new)

> *C'est une **jeune** femme moderne, mais elle ne kiffe que les **vieux** trucs vintage!*
> She's a **young**, modern woman, but she only likes **old** vintage things!

Number: *autre* (other) *un* (one), *deux* (two) …

> *J'ai **deux** soeurs, **un** qui étudie aux États-Unis, et **l'autre** qui bosse à Singapour.*
> I have **two** sisters, **one** who studies in the US, the **other** who works in Singapore.

Goodness: *bon/bonne* (good), *meilleur(e)* (better), *gentil/gentille* (nice/sweet), *grand(e)* (great), *mauvais(e)* (bad), *faux/fausse* (fake)

> *Je sais que tu es une **bonne** personne.*
> I know you're a **good** person.

12

Size: *grand(e)* (big, tall), *haut(e)* (high), *petit(e)* (small, little), *gros/grosse* (large/fat), *court(e)* (short), *long/longue* (long)

> *Prends la **petite** ruelle à gauche, après tu verras une **grosse** statue de marbre, et c'est juste à côté.*
> Take the **little** street to the left, after you'll see a **big** marble statue, and it's right next to that.

Adverbs are *generally* formed by taking the feminine form of the adjective and adding *-ment*. For example:

> quick/quickly
> *rapide/rapidement*

However, as always, there are exceptions to the rule. For example:

> good/well
> *bonne/bien*

> bad/badly
> *mauvaise/mal*

Adverbs typically follow the verb, except the commonly used/shorter ones that precede it. For example:

> *Pardon, je t'ai **mal** entendu.*
> Sorry, I heard you **badly**.

> *Tu l'as **bien** cuisiné.*
> You cooked it **well**.

How to Form a Question

There are several ways to ask for information. The simplest/ most common way to ask a question is to add the phrase *Est-ce que* (is it that) to a statement.

> **Are you** hungry?
> ***Est-ce que*** *t'as faim?*
> Literally, "Is it that you're hungry?"

Put that phrase in between a question word and the sentence: *Qui* (Who), *Que* ("What" with something following), *Où* (Where), *Quand* (When), *Pourquoi* (Why), *Comment* (How). For example:

> ***Qu'est-ce que*** *tu veux faire?*
> **What** do you want to do?

> ***Où est-ce qu'****on va?*
> **Where** are we going?

Invert the verb and the subject: *As-tu faim?* (Are you hungry?). In some situations, using inversion can make you sound that much more *sophistiquée* (sophisticated).

Saying the statement with inquisitive intonation, placing the emphasis on the end, is a more casual way to form a question.

> *T'as* **faim**?
> Are you **hungry**?

> *T'habites* **où**?
> **Where** do you live?

Add the phrase *n'est-ce pas?* (isn't that right?) at the end.

> *T'as faim, **n'est-ce pas**?*
> You're hungry, **right**?

> *T'habites à Paris, **n'est-ce pas**?*
> You live in Paris, **right**?

How to Negate a Sentence

To negate a sentence you simply put a *ne* in front of the verb and a *pas* directly after. Anytime you use the negation phrase, you turn the action from affirmative to negative, like the English "don't." For example:

> I like Paris.
> *J'aime Paris.*

> I don't like Paris.
> *Je n'aime pas Paris.*
> Again, see how the *ne* in front of the *aime* becomes *n'aime*. Side-by side vowels like that are often contracted.

Slang vs. Formal

As sophisticated as French is, its native speakers have a very elaborate slang that you'll be tapping into with this book. It's important to note, however, that they have an old-school mind-set in terms of addressing their elders, bosses, teachers, doctors, etc. These "highly respectable" types must be addressed differently than your friends or someone younger than you. Same goes for people you don't know.

Grammatically (consult a grammar guide for in-depth rules)
there's a separate verb conjugation for this situation. It's
the same as the *vous* (you plural) conjugation. Here are the
conjugations for the really important verbs "to be" (*être*),
"to have" (*avoir*), and "to do" (*faire*). The first two are used in
conjugating more complex tenses, including the past tense.
Faire is used for actions like: *faire du shopping* (to shop),
weather terms like *il fait chaud/froid* (it's hot/cold), and more.

être—to be

je suis	I am	*nous sommes*	we are
tu es	you are (informal)	*vous êtes*	you are (plural or formal)
il/elle/on est	he/she/one is	*ils/elles sont*	they are

> **You're** really smart.
> ***T'es*** très intelligent. *(informal)* ***Vous êtes*** très
> intelligent. *(formal)*
> Again, if the person is a woman, add an "e" or for *vous*
> plural add an "e" (women), an "s," or both. Adjectives
> must always agree with the noun.

avoir—to have

j'ai	I have	*nous avons*	we have
tu as	you have (informal)	*vous avez*	you have (plural or formal)
il/elle/on a	he/she/one has	*ils/elles ont*	they have

D'ya got any dough? (informal) vs. **Do you have**
any money? (formal)
T'as *du fric?* (informal) **Avez-vous** *de l'argent?*
(formal)

faire—to make/do/play

je fais	I do	*nous faisons*	we do
tu fais	you do (informal)	*vous faisez*	you do (plural or formal)
il/elle/ on fait	he/she/one does	*ils/elles font*	they do

Me, **I'm playing** tennis, what **are you doing**?
Moi, **fais du** *tennis, qu'est-ce que* **vous faites**?
(formal)

You'll also note that younger people use a lot of
abbreviations and contractions in their speech. This might
make it a bit harder to understand your friends at first, but
eventually you'll catch on.

Often they conjoin vowels that are next to each other,
making the speech a truncated short form. Most common
is in addressing each other with those two first verbs *être*
and *avoir*. Rather than enunciating the *tu es/tu as* (you are/
you have) you'll just see *t'es/t'as*. This is how it's written
throughout the book since this is a slang guide, but in
a formal situation, refer to the proper conjugation. For
example:

You have to do what today?
T'as quoi à faire aujourd'hui?

You're so hot, sweetie.
T'es canon, chérie.

In a negative statement they will often omit the *ne* part of the *ne...pas* negation. For example:

I **don't** want your help.
*Je **ne** veux **pas** ton aide. (formal) Je veux **pas** ton aide. (informal)*

There's a second slang form called *verlan* that follows similar ideas to pig latin, where all the words are inversed (*verlan* is the inverse of *à l'envers*, which means "backward") except it's used heavily and is actually cool. Basically they take commonly used words and invert them to be "unintelligible" to the uncool peeps around them. Except now it's so omnipresent that most words are recognizable. The *verlan* vocab grows constantly, but here are some mainstays:

femme/meuf
woman

mec/keum
guy

flic/keuf
cop

fou/ouf
crazy (cool)

louche/chelou
sketchy

lourd/relou
heavy (beats for example) or boring (people)

photo/tof
photo

métro/trom
subway

Introducing yourself
TE PRÉSENTER

So now that you've put those rouged lips to work trying to adapt to the French way of speaking, it's time for your grand *début* into Parisian society. You aren't going to be fluent anytime soon if you don't get out there and start talking to people. The more you immerse yourself into a culture, the more your proficiency in the language will grow. Challenge yourself to speak it as much as possible. Don't shut down the second some cutie asks you for directions on the street. Listen carefully and try your best to respond. If you really aren't comfortable, simply admit that *Pardon, je ne parle pas français* (Sorry, I don't speak French). At least not yet you don't. Dip your toe in and start simple with the *hey girl heys* and the *how do you dos*? It's a fast track to Frenchified fabulosity ...

Greetings SALUTATIONS

Hello
Bonjour

Hey
Salut

Good morning/day/
afternoon
Bonjour

Good evening
Bonsoir

Good night
Bonne nuit

How are you, Mr./Mrs./
Miss Lenoir? (formal)
*Comment allez-vous, Monsieur/Madame/Mademoiselle
Lenoir?*

How are you?
Comment tu vas?

What's up?
Ça va?

Very well, thank you.
Très bien, merci.

All good / I'm good.
Ça va bien.

Not so good.
Pas très bien.

So-so.
Comme-ci comme-ça.

And you? (informal/formal)
Et toi/vous?

Long time no see!
Ça fait longtemps!

What's new with you? (informal/formal)
Quoi de neuf? / Qu'est-ce que vous devenez?

Nothing new/special.
Rien de nouveau/de spécial.

Same ol' shit.
Toujours le même bordel.

Introductions INTRODUCTIONS

Hey ...
Salut ...

My name is Lara.
Je m'appelle Lara.

I'm from Chicago / America.
Je viens de Chicago / des États-Unis.

I'm 23 years old.
J'ai 23 ans.
Literally, "I have 23 years."

I'm a student.
Je suis étudiante.

It's nice to meet you. (informal/formal)
Enchantée de te/vous rencontrer.

Good-bye AU REVOIR

Keep me in the loop.
Tiens-moi au jus.

Tell me.
Dis-le-moi.

Let me know.
Fais-moi savoir.

Call me.
Appelle-moi.

Text me.
Envoie-moi un texto.

Good-bye.
Au revoir.

Bye.
Salut.

See ya.
Ciao.

See you later.
À plus tard.

Later.
À plus.

See you tomorrow.
À demain.

See you soon.
À bientôt.

Manners
LES BONNES MANIÈRES

Excuse me. (informal/formal)
Excuse-moi/Excusez-moi.

I'm sorry to bother you ...what time is it?
Excusez-moi de vous déranger ...quelle heure est-il?
Any time you interrupt a stranger to ask them a question, it's best to start with the first half of this sentence.

Pardon
Pardon
When you bump into someone accidentally, simply say this.

Sorry
Désolée

Sorry, I don't speak French.
Désolée, je ne parle pas français.

Do you speak English?
Parlez-vous anglais?

Please speak slower.
Parlez plus lentement, s'il vous plaît.

Please repeat that.
Répétez cela, s'il vous plaît.

I am sorry (for being late).
Je suis désolée (d'être en retard).

Please. (informal/formal)
S'il te/vous plaît.

Thanks.
Merci.

Thank you very much.
Merci beaucoup.

Chapter 2

Daily Life:
La Vie Quotidienne

"There is but one Paris and however hard living may be here, the French air clears the mind and does a lot of good—a world of good."

—VINCENT VAN GOGH

The most fun you can have in Paris is when you actually play *parisienne*. As in living like a native and not being an obvious tourist, as adorable as you might be. Try to understand the lay of the land and the lifestyle that follows. Navigating the City of Lights isn't difficult in the least as long as you know what to expect. Simply have an open mind, take your time, and challenge yourself. Don't just marvel at the beauty of an iconic structure that's on your "must-see" list and call it a day. Everything in your new world is worth acknowledging, and the more aware you are of your glittering surroundings, the more familiar you'll be with the city in general. So as you unwind to take in the loveliness, slow your roll in general. The French treasure their free time and live it up in full; working 24/7 isn't really a national priority. Initially you might find this to be an inconvenience, but eventually you'll cherish the slower pace. All the better to stop and smell the roses with, darling.

Weather LE TEMPS

As you're meandering about Paris and you look around, you'll notice a lovely palette of blackly clad beauties walking along stark white architecture. Now turn your attention upward and admire how the sky is a perfect mélange of the two—chances are it's gray. People typically don't come to Paris for the weather. The winters are mild and it doesn't snow often, but don't be surprised if the second an inch of white drops the entire city shuts down. Likewise, the sun doesn't really shine other than in the summer and sporadically during fall and spring. The frequent showers are also part of the Parisian charm, I promise. But maybe check the forecast before you debut any new suede shoes. Just tuck a cute lil' *parapluie* (umbrella) in your bag, babycakes, and nothing will rain on your parade.

What's the weather? I hope it's nice out.
Quel temps fait-il? J'espère qu'il fait beau.

It's ...
Il fait ...

> hot.
> *chaud.*

> humid.
> *humide.*

> cool.
> *frais.*

cold.
froid.

It's ...
Il y a ...

foggy.
du brouillard.

sunny.
du soleil.

windy.
du vent.

I'm so tired of this shitty weather! It's ...
J'en ai marre de ce temps de merde. Il ...

freezing.
gèle.

pouring.
pleut des cordes.
Literally, "raining ropes."

raining.
pleut.

snowing.
neige.

Time L'HEURE

In Europe they run on the 24-hour clock, so if you aren't familiar with it, telling time will be a little mathematical for you initially. Minutes past the hour until the half hour are added directly to the hour. However, past halfway of the hour you can either subtract from the next hour on the 12-hour clock, or add minutes to the 24-hour clock as usual. The French also use an "h" for *heure* (hour) instead of a colon when writing time. In terms of punctuality, the French are on time at the earliest but generally a little bit behind. It's not a product of rudeness or nonchalance—they don't come early simply out of respect for the host's wishes. It's best to give him/her some extra time for preparation rather than shortchange their efforts to impress. Embrace the extra minutes and know that being fashionably late is totally *à la mode*!

What time is it?
Il est quelle heure?

It's ...
Il est ...

> 9 a.m.
> *neuf heures (9h).*
>
> noon.
> *midi (12h).*

1:15 p.m.
treize heures quinze/une heure et quart (13h15).
To say a quarter past you say the 12-hour figure and then
add *et quart* (and a quarter).

3:30 p.m.
quinze heures trente/trois heures et demie (15h30).
To indicate the halfway point, you can either say the 30
minutes, *trente* (thirty), or add *et demie* (and a half).

5:45 p.m.
*dix-sept heures quartante-cinq/six heures moins le
quart (17h45).*
To subtract minutes from the hour put *moins* (minus) in
front of the remaining minutes to the next hour.

6:37 p.m.
dix-huit heures trente-sept (18h37).

7:55 p.m.
*dix-neuf heures cinquante-cinq/huit heures moins
cinq (19h55).*

10:12 p.m.
vingt-deux heures douze (22h12).

midnight.
minuit/zéro-heure.

Here are the numbers 1 to 24:

one	*un, une (heure)*
two	*deux*
three	*trois*
four	*quatre*
five	*cinq*
six	*six*
seven	*sept*
eight	*huit*
nine	*neuf*
ten	*dix*
eleven	*onze*
twelve	*douze (midi)*
thirteen	*treize*
fourteen	*quatorze*
fifteen	*quinze*
sixteen	*seize*
seventeen	*dix-sept*
eighteen	*dix-huit*
nineteen	*dix-neuf*
twenty	*vingt*
twenty-one	*vingt-et-un*
twenty-two	*vingt-deux*
twenty-three	*vingt-trois*
twenty-four	*vingt-quatre (minuit)*

Hey Nadia, you're...
Salut Nadia, t'es ...

You should get there ...
Tu devrais te pointer ...

>early (arrival).
>*en avance.*

>early (in the day).
>*tôt.*

>late (not on time).
>*en retard.*

>late (in the evening).
>*tard.*

>on time.
>*à l'heure.*

>on time (sharp).
>*pile à l'heure.*

Getting Around BOUGER

A great thing about Paris is that regardless of it being a big city, it's entirely walkable! You can easily sashay about from *quartier* to *quartier* (hood to hood) but chances are you won't really have to. Each neighborhood is developed enough that you'll find everything you need within a delightful little radius. Don't throw your stilettos on just yet though. Most of the streets are charmingly old-school, so you'll be navigating cobblestones and uneven sidewalks most of the time. Moreover, a shortcut can turn into a really elongated escapade as the city has many winding streets and alleyways. However, once you get your *rues* and *ruelles* down you'll feel like a true *Parisienne*. Nothing beats the ability to give directions as a foreigner.

Excuse me, I'm looking for a/an ...
Excusez-moi, je cherche un/une ...

Where's the nearest ...?
Où est le/la ... plus proche?

Where is the ... of the neighborhood?
Où est le/la .... du coin?

> ATM
> *un/le distributeur (automatique)*
>
> bank
> *une/la banque*
>
> city hall
> *la mairie*
> A *mairie* in Paris is where all the governmental action takes place in each arrondissement. So the *mairie* of the 5th *arrondissement* is *La Mairie du Cinquième.*
>
> library
> *une/la biblio*

post office
une/la poste

pharmacy
une/la pharmacie

metro stop
un/le métro

train station
une/la gare
The six main train stations in Paris are (clockwise): Gare
Saint-Lazare, Gare du Nord, Gare de l'Est, Gare de Lyon,
Gare d'Austerlitz, and Gare Montparnasse.

Is it far?
C'est loin?

How far is it to...?
À quelle distance est...?

It's really far. Take the metro.
C'est très loin. Prends le métro.

And which way do I go again?
Et j'y vais par où déjà?

How do I get there?
J'y vais comment?

Which direction?
Quelle direction?

At the corner
Au coin

A few streets after the next one
Quelques rues plus loin

Three blocks away
À trois rues d'ici

An hour by foot
À une heure à pied

To the corner then ...
Au coin de la rue et puis ...

> straight ahead.
> *tout droit.*

> to the left.
> *à gauche.*

> to the right.
> *à droite.*

> across from ...
> *en face de ...*

> in front of ...
> *devant ...*

> next to ...
> *à côté de ...*

behind.
derrière.

up.
en haut.

down.
en bas.

north.
au nord.

south.
au sud.

west.
à l'ouest.

east.
à l'est.

Public Transport
LES TRANSPORTS PUBLICS

Despite the fact that the French aren't huge fans of "working" per se, they've got an incredibly efficient transportation system. The national commuters' mantra is *métro-boulot-dodo* (metro-job-bedtime) and as such, the metro plays an integral part of *la vie quotidienne*. Within the *RATP* (Parisian public transport system) there are also buses, the RER commuter rail to suburbs like Versailles, and trams. These will get you from place to place in no time. Moreover, each station has a constantly updated digital schedule to make your commute all the more timely. The point is you've got endless options in terms of your Parisian wheels, so feel free to cruise them all!

I don't feel like walking. Let's take a ... there.
J'ai pas envie de marcher. On prend un..

We missed the last train. We need to find the nearest ...
On a raté le dernier métro. On doit trouver le/la ... le/la plus proche.

bus, bus stop
le bus, l'arrêt de bus
The buses in Paris are very clean, comprehensive, and reliable. Whereas the metro will be full of Parisians and tourists alike, the buses are pretty much natives only. They cover a lot of ground in the city, so many commuters take buses to school or work. They have the same ticket system as *le métro*; tickets can be purchased in any metro station, but not onboard. You can buy single tickets, a book (*carnet*) of ten, or a 1/2/3/5 day *Paris Visite* pass. For longer stays, get a Navigo smart card at main stations.

late night bus
le Noctilien
These are the night buses that operate on limited hours in the interim when the metro's closed. They run about every

half hour, so you might be better off just partying on and waiting for the first morning train.

cab, cab stand
un/le taxi, une/la station de taxi
In terms of taxis, if you can't just flag 'em down on the street NYC-style, there are curbside taxi stations everywhere.

city bike sharing
le Vélib
Many Parisians, day or night, utilize the public bike rental system called *Vélib* to jet around the city (first 30 minutes free!). *Vélib* stops, and their detailed area maps, are a great secret to orienting yourself when you're frolicking about the city. You can get tickets online or obtain a card if you're going to use it often.

subway
le métro
With 16 lines and over 300 stations, including the world's largest *Châtelet-Les Halles*, the Paris subway system is as impressive as it is extensive. The system might seem daunting to someone not used to public transportation, but almost all signs are in French and English, and the maps within the station will help orient yourself in an unfamiliar area. On some lines you've got to push the handle upward to exit, while others have automatic doors.

tram
le tram
Trams run around the periphery of the city at street level.

suburban train
le RER
The RER is a commuter rail to suburbs like Versailles and the airports. These will get you from place to place in no time.

You live near / work at which ...?
T'habites / Tu bosses près de quel(le) ...?

bus stop
arrêt (de bus)

metro stop
station (de métro)

metro line
ligne de métro

Traveling LE VOYAGE

As lovely as Paris is, if you have the luxury, travel around France or Europe in your spare time. The beauty of Europe is that nations are super close together; going from country to country is like state hopping for Americans. You're just hours away from a whole new language, culture, and people. Now, don't think all this jet-setting has to be a costly affair, darling. Easyjet and Hop! can fly you from country to country at criminally low prices, and Eurolines is the bus equivalent. European trains are super fast and crazy comfortable, so if you want a more scenic route, give that a whirl. The SNCF handles all of the French domestic train connections, and the Eurostar will get you from Paris to London in only 2h15! Treat yourself *à l'anglaise* (with English style), have a shopping spree and tea, and be back in Paris by nighttime. Hostels and apartment rentals in Europe can be quite stylish as well, so there's no need to be spendy on hotels, unless of course you wanna luxe it up. Aim to pack light—you know you'll want some souvenirs for your

intercultural closet. Buy yourself a ticket and give that passport some long overdue lovin'. The world is your oyster, babe, and it's blinging real bright.

Girl, I'm in serious need of some R & R. I wanna go to Saint Tropez.
Meuf, j'ai trop besoin du repos. Je veux aller à Saint Tropez.

Let's take a vacation ...
Prenons des vacances ...

Spring break's soon. How about ...?
C'est bientôt les vacances de printemps. Ça te dit ...?

> traveling around France
> *de faire un tour en province*

> backpacking in Eastern Europe
> *de voyager avec un sac à dos en Europe de l'Est*

> going somewhere with a beach
> *d'aller quelquepart avec une plage*

> going to London
> *d'aller à Londres*

> going to Morocco
> *d'aller au Maroc*

> going to Spain
> *d'aller en Espagne*

> going to Africa
> *d'aller en Afrique*

In terms of geographical prepositions, to say "to"—for cities: à; masculine countries: *"au"*; and for the feminine/masculine ones that begin with a vowel: *"en."*

At the airport *À l'aéroport*

Okay, sweetie, the plane leaves in two hours. Where is/ are ...?
D'accord, ma puce, l'avion décolle en deux heures. Où est/ sont ...?

> the boarding gate
> *la porte d'embarquement*
>
> the check-in
> *l'enregistrement*
>
> customs
> *la douane*
>
> the luggage
> *les bagages*
>
> the tickets (one-way/round-trip)
> *les billets (aller-simple/aller-retour)*
>
> the terminal
> *le terminal*
>
> security check
> *les contrôles de sécurité*
>
> your passport
> *ton passeport*

At the hotel *À l'hôtel*

Hello, I would like a room ...
Bonjour, je voudrais une chambre ...

> for two people.
> *pour deux personnes.*

> for three nights.
> *pour trois nuits.*

> with a double bed/two beds.
> *avec un grand lit/à deux lits.*

> with a view.
> *avec une vue.*

> with a W.C./full bathroom.
> *avec un W.C./une salle de bain.*

With French lodging there is the option of having a room with a shared or private W.C. (toilet and sink) or a full bathroom with shower/tub as well. The W.C. is typically cheaper, so the preference depends on your needs.

At Reception *À La Reception*

Good evening, Sir, I would like ...
Bonsoir, Monsieur, j'aimerais ...

> an 8 a.m. wake-up call.
> *être réveillée à huit heures (8h).*

44

✄

to check-out.
faire mon check-out.

to pay my bill (in cash/with credit).
régler ma facture en espèces/avec une carte de crédit.

Do you have ...?
Avez-vous ...?

air-conditioning
la climatisation

continental breakfast
un petit déjeuner continental

an elevator
un ascenseur

laundry service
un service de lessive

a neighborhood/city map
un plan du quartier/de la ville

a pool
une piscine

any restaurant recommendations
des conseils pour un restaurant

Neighborhood Guide
GUIDE DES ARRONDISSEMENTS

You've heard how Paris is picture-perfect in all respects, but part of its charm really lies within its metropolitan variance. The paramount feature of the Parisian landscape is the Seine, a river that splits the city into two large sections, the Left Bank *(Rive Gauche)* to the South and Right Bank *(Rive Droite)* to the North. In addition to the two banks, the city is more commonly divided into 20 neighborhoods called *les arrondissements*. They're organized in the shape of a snail, spiraling out clockwise from the middle of the city, and often referred to by number. Each *quartier* (neighborhood) exudes a very different vibe; exploring every one of them is part of the experience, darling. Your new stomping ground awaits some serious hotfooting. Here's what loveliness lies ahead.

Le premier, 1er: Le Louvre/ Palais Royal

THE ultimate tourist's haven, the Louvre, Palais Royal, and Les Halles, etc., make for endless sightseeing and shopping to be had. No worries, babe, when your tootsies need a rest, the beautiful *Jardin des Tuileries* is a majestic garden that allows you to sightsee in a different manner. Sit on a lounge chair, marvel at the pretty passers-by, and enjoy the scenic backdrop.

Arrondissements

1 Le premier, 1er: Le Louvre/ Palais Royal
2 Le deuxième, 2ème: Bourse
3 Le troisième, 3ème: Le (Haut) Marais
4 Le quatrième, 4ème: Le Marais
5 Le cinquième, 5ème: Le Quartier Latin
6 Le sixième, 6ème: Saint-Germain-des-Prés
7 Le septième, 7ème: La Tour Eiffel
8 Le huitième, 8ème: Champs-Élysées
9 Le neuvième, 9ème: Opéra, Pigalle
10 Le dixième, 10ème: Canal Saint Martin
11 Le onzième, 11ème: Bastille
12 Le douzième, 12ème: Bercy
13 Le treizième, 13ème: Place d'Italie
14 Le quatorzième, 14ème: Vaugirard
15 Le quinzème, 15ème: Parc des Expositions
16 Le seizième, 16ème: Trocadéro/ Passy
17 Le dix-septième, 17ème: Batignolles- Monceau
18 Le dix-huitième, 18ème: Montmartre
19 Le dix-neuvième, 19ème: Parc de la Villette
20 Le vingtième, 20ème: Belleville

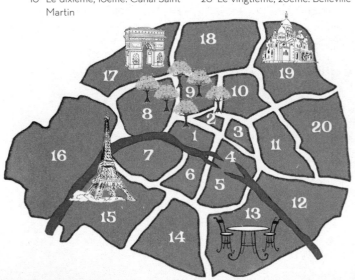

Le deuxième, 2ème: Bourse

Historically, *le deuxième* is primarily a business zone, with the stock market, countless peeps in suits, and a whole lot of money floating around. However, recently the hood has been gentrifying with young *bobo (bohemian-bourgeois)* families moving in. With the numerous resto-bars scattered around the *Boulevard Poissonière*, the *2ème* lights up as the ties loosen and the debauchery unfolds.

Le troisième, 3ème: Le (Haut) Marais

This is the more untouched northern half of the hippest hood in Paris, *Le Marais*. There's a myriad of shops, cafés, and galleries sprinkled throughout, and the oldest market in Paris, *Le marché des enfants rouges*, dating back to 1615. Once resided by the city's noblest families, the area boasts 17th century mansions and is now home to the Picasso Museum and *le Musée Carnavelet*, among other cultural institutions.

Le quatrième, 4ème: Le Marais

This historically Jewish area, centered around *la rue des Rosiers*, still has some beautiful temples and fancy falafel to its name. Today it's teeming with trendy shops, bars, and a fantastic gay nightlife scene. It's the perfect spot for brunching, boozing, and boutiquing. The gorgeous *Place des Vosges* is the city's oldest square, and the contemporary art center, *Le Centre Pompidou,* isn't too far off. Meander two of the Seine's isles, pick up some famed *Berthillon* ice cream on the *Île Saint-Louis*, and have the Notre Dame Cathedral amaze you on the *Île de la Cité*.

Le cinquième, 5ème: Le Quartier Latin

The 5ème's *Université de la Sorbonne* once taught scholars in the common language of Latin, hence the name. Now it's the land of inexpensive cafés, bookstores, student bars, and cinemas galore. Not to be missed is *La Mosquée de Paris*; the Parisian mosque/bathhouse/open-air café where birds flutter about and traditional tea treats are served. It's a lovely nod to the city's Muslim influence.

Le sixième, 6ème: Saint-Germain-des-Prés

Le Boulevard Saint-Germain traverses the three northern arrondissements of the Left Bank. It has always been an intellectual haunt, attracting writers, artists, and philosophers alike to exchange ideas over drawn-out coffee seshes. It was also the birthplace of Existentialism. Two famed adjacent cafés, *Les Deux Magots* and *Le Café de Flore*, are as popular now as ever. The hood is very posh, with specialty boutiques and pricey resto-bars everywhere. The luscious *Jardin du Luxembourg* adds a nice escape.

Le septième, 7ème: La Tour Eiffel

The emblem of all things Parisian and chic, here struts *la Tour Eiffel*. A gritty iron queen by day and a lit-up glamour girl at night, her iconic splendor towers over the sprawling *Champs de Mars*, a former military lawn. The *Musée d'Orsay*, a former neoclassical train station turned impressionist art museum sits right alongside *la Seine,* as does the *Musée Rodin.* Likewise, *le rue Clèr* is one of the best market streets in Paris!

Le huitième, 8ème: Champs-Élysées

Surely you've heard of the grandiose retail boulevard *les Champs-Élysées.* From shops on shops on shops to resto chains to luxe clubs, everything is bigger and blingier on *les Champs.* It connects two landmarks, the *Place de L'Étoile* and the *Place de la Concorde.* These squares feature major monuments like *l'Arc de Triomphe,* a 3,400-year-old Egyptian obelisk, eight female statues embodying French cities, and a host of other historical goodies. *Place de la Concorde* is also where Marie Antoinette had her perfectly coiffed head offed.

Le neuvième, 9ème: Opéra, Pigalle

This diverse neighborhood is a mix of two pretty different vibes. The Southern part, *Opéra,* revolves around business and commerce, with the *Grand Opéra* and *les Grands Magasins* (the big department stores) running along *Boulevard Haussmann.* On the other hand, up north in Pigalle you'll find the bygone era of *Le Moulin Rouge* and a gritty arts scene. This area is a treasure trove of cafés, concerts, and underground galleries.

Le dixième, 10ème: Canal Saint-Martin

The hood's appeal centers around the elongated and energetic *Canal Saint-Martin.* It's the perfect setting for waterside picnics, bike rides, or some serious urban bronzing. All the restos, bars, and shops lining the canal offer lots of day-to-night fun. Life is served on a multicultural platter here, so expect diversity in both the edible and aesthetic sense. Two main train stations, the *Gare de L'est* and *Gare du Nord* are also in the 10ème.

Le onzième, 11ème: Bastille

Named after *la Place de la Bastille*, this is the iconic site where the Bastille prison once stood and was stormed during the French Revolution. The new opera and several concert halls are in the area, hence a rather bustling entertainment scene. Check the *rue de la Roquette* and *rue Oberkampf* for all the night crawlers.

Le douzième, 12ème: Bercy

This area is pretty industrial but there are some charming attractions too. You've got all the railways of the *Gare de Lyon* and the event epicenter *Palais Omnisports de Paris-Bercy*. For those who enjoy long walks in the park, the *Parc de Bercy*, a lush, manicured meadow beside the *Palais*, and *le Coulée Verte*, an elevated garden spanning the entire hood will offer a nice urban repos. Cultureheads will enjoy *le Musée de la Cinémathèque Française* for some cinematic history, as well as *Le Viaduct des Arts*, a former railroad viaduct turned gallery row.

Le treizième, 13ème: Place d'Italie

Largely a multiethnic residential spot, including Paris's Chinatown, recent developments have turned the area into a pretty hip hood. *La Seine* is on its eastern border, and taking advantage of the waterside vistas, clubs and restos are cropping up along the docks. *Gare d'Austerlitz* (a main train station) calls the *13ème* home too.

Le quatorzième, 14ème: Vaugirard

Full of students from neighboring universities, there are tons of cafés, inexpensive delis, and clubs nearby. *Boulevard Montparnasse* is a huge shopping thoroughfare, which adds a more commercial appeal. Finally, with the *Gare Montparnasse* and *Tour Montparnasse* (skyscraper with viewing deck), there are lots of tourists and commuters frolicking about.

Le quinzième, 15ème: Parc des Expositions

This neighborhood is primarily residential, and is notably the city's most populous *arrondissement*. Adjacent to the *7ème*, the *15ème* still has prime views of the Eiffel Tower and you can enjoy being along the Seine.

Le seizième, 16ème: Trocadéro/Passy

New York's Fifth Avenue is to *les Champs-Élysées* as Park Avenue is to the *16ème*, except in neighborhood form. This posh area has BMWs and Birkins around every perfectly manicured corner. The *rue de Passy* is full of high-end shopping and classy cafés for the ladies who lunch. The

Place du Trocadéro esplanade boasts a museum, a theater, and a garden. Directly across *la Seine* from the Eiffel Tower, it's the perfect spot for a photo op!

Le dix-septième, 17ème: Batignolles-Monceau

The *Batignolles* neighborhood has a two-sided nature. Its upscale element branches off *les Champs*, with lots of luxury hotels and restaurants littered about. However, more north you'll find a sizeable ethnic community. Historically, the *17ème* was frequented by impressionist painter Édouard Manet and his friends, called the *"groupe des Batignolles."* They were inspired by the *quartier's* cultural vibrancy that still resonates today.

Le dix-huitième, 18ème: Montmartre

Situated atop a hill, this is where the famed *le Sacré Coeur* sits pretty, overlooking the whole city. It was the home of the bohemian art scene in the 19th century, attracting the likes of Van Gogh, Matisse, Renoir, and Degas with its creative pulse and lively cabarets. While its current inhabitants might not have the same prestige as its previous ones, there is still a vibrant artistic air wafting through the winding roads.

Le dix-neuvième, 19ème: Parc de la Villette

The *19ème* is a residential area boasting a lot of diversity in its local shops, restaurants, and two major parks. The *Parc des Buttes-Chaumont* is a luscious hilltop forest that illuminates in the summer with organized parties. The *Parc de la Villette* is a massive greenspace that is the foundation for Europe's largest science museum, *la Cité des Sciences et de l'Industrie,* the Parisian Philharmonic, and several other entertainment institutions.

Le vingtième, 20ème: Belleville

The word *Belleville* means beautiful town, and its allure lies in its artistic multiculturalism. The area's biggest attraction is the *Cimetière Père Lachaise,* an enormous cemetery hosting the ashes of many iconic French artists, writers, and public figures. The *Parc de Belleville* is the city's highest park, and with sweeping views of Paris, it's a wonderful perch for a summer evening.

Chapter 3

Friendship: L'Amitié

"A girl without a friend is like the springtime without roses."

—ADRIEN DE MONTLUC

While you might think the best souvenir from your trip to Paris is a suitcase full of fabulous clothes, nothing will complete it like a new friend. This might seem obvious, but it is no easy feat, my dear. While Americans are rather open with one another and could gab with a perfect stranger for days, the French are kinda the opposite. Don't write them off as rude or insular—they're simply more conservative with their personal lives than we are. You want to take that darling Frenchie who sits next to you in class to a café? It will happen, but all in due time. And when it does she'll tour you around and make you experience her city *à la parisienne* (as Parisians do). Likewise, our mantra to "make yourselves at home" or *fais comme chez toi* might only extend to the living room. People can be friends for decades without ever seeing the entire abodes of their *amies* (friends). That being said, as your relationship deepens and they open up both their homes and hearts, it will be a friendship that long outlives your Parisian stay.

Personality Types
TYPES DE PERSONNALITÉ

Urban myths often depict the *Parisienne* as this flawlessly chic and immortal being, divine in her own right. She's also human and comes in every shape, size, and demeanor. From sweet to sassy to downright sour, she can have it all behind that charming little aura she's got goin' on. Note that the "politically correct" American standard isn't a global phenomenon, so if something comes out a bit *off*, don't discredit the person immediately; simply consider it a potential cultural distinction. They're pretty unfiltered in what they say and very nonchalant in their actions. Likewise, whereas in America we're a very expressive, encouraging and open-minded culture, the French are more of a reserved mind-set. There are many of those delightful differences, so take them in stride. Don't judge any of your new acquaintances by their covers—peruse the pages and hopefully you'll add a new friend to your library.

Hey, let me introduce you to ...
Tiens, je te présente ...

> my friend (f).
> *mon amie, ma copine/pote.*
>
> my friend (m).
> *mon ami/copain/pote.*
>
> my best friend.
> *ma meilleure + amie/copine/pote.*

bestie.
my best.
As this is an anglicized term, you use "my" instead of *mon/ma.*

collegue.
mon/ma collègue (m/f).

aquaintance.
une connaissance (m/f).

You know my new **friend** Camille? She's really ...
*Tu connais ma nouvelle **copine** Camille? Elle est grave...*
The verb *connaître* means "to know" in terms of a person or a place.
Something you can be familiar with. The verb *savoir* means to know
in terms of factual information. Example: It's crazy I've known her for
10 years, but I don't know where she lives. *(C'est dingue, ca fait 10
ans que je la connais, mais je sais pas où elle habite.)*

charming.
charmante.

chatty.
bavarde.

chill.
tranquille.

clever.
maligne.

cool.
branchée.
Branchée is "cool" like hip and "in the know." Plain old
"cool" is *cool.*

58

crazy.
dingue/ouf.

fun.
fun.

funny.
marrante.

loyal.
loyale.

nice.
sympa.

smart.
intelligente.

sweet.
adorable.

witty.
pleine d'esprit.

What a **frenemy** Léa is. Turns out she's pretty ...
*Qu'est-ce qu'elle est **faux-jeton**, Léa. Il se trouve qu'elle est vachement ...*

annoying.
chiante.

back-stabbing.
faux-cul.

bitchy/catty.
garce.

ditzy.
neuneu.

dumb.
bête.

hopeless.
nulle.
You can also be *nulle* (useless) at something. Example: *Elle est nulle en cuisine.* (She's a bad cook.)

naïve.
naïve.

prissy.
prude.

selfish.
égoïste.

slutty.
salope.

spoiled.
gâtée.

I got in a fight with Louise, the little ...
Je me suis embrouillée avec Louise, la petite ...

bitch.
salope.
Interchangeable for "whore."

cow.
vache.

cunt.
conne.

whore.
pute.

fucker.
connasse.

liar.
mytho.

slut.
pétasse.

Playdates
SORTIES ENTRE COPINES

From five-hour café seshes to shopping sprees, Paris is the perfect playland for a friendship to blossom. Be bold and try new places, *arrondissements*, restaurants, anything. Experimenting and exploring your new city will be twice as fun with someone to share it with. Now that you've got a new partner in crime, let's get you *filles* (girls) frolicking!

Girl, I miss you, we gotta **catch up!** C'mon let's ...
Meuf, tu me manques trop, faut qu'on **se capte***! Allez, on ...*
Il faut que takes the subjunctive and is a common phrase meaning "it's necessary that/to." The *il* is often neglected orally.

> chill at a café.
> *se pose au troquet.*
>
> get a coffee.
> *se prenne un café.*
>
> get a drink.
> *se prenne un pot.*
>
> go catch a movie.
> *se fasse un cinoche.*
>
> go out!
> *sorte!*
>
> go shopping.
> *se fasse du shopping.*
>
> grab a bite.
> *mange un morceau.*
>
> have dinner together.
> *dîne ensemble.*
>
> have a picnic!
> *se fasse un pique-nique!*

take a walk.
fasse une balade.

Okay, tell me about your ...
D'accord, raconte-moi ton/ta ...

big surprise!
grande nouvelle (f)!

childhood.
enfance (f).

day.
journée (f).

Tell me about your ...
Parle-moi de ton/ta ...

boss.
boss/chef (m/f).

boyfriend.
copain/petit ami.

girlfriend.
copine.

job.
taf (m).

life.
vie (f).

problems.
problèmes (mpl).

roommates.
collocs (m/fpl).

vacay!
vacances (fpl)!

Did you have a good **weekend,** darling? What'd ya do?
*T'as passée un bon **weekend,** chouchou? T'as fait quoi?*

I ...
Je/J' ...
If the verb that immediately follows the *Je* (I) begins with a vowel,
you contract it. Otherwise you leave it as is.

had a really great **date**!
*ai eu un **rancard** super sympa!*

had a friend in town visiting.
avais un ami en ville qui m'a rendu visite.

slept in.
ai fait la grasse matinée.

did absolutely nothing. I was sooo lazy.
ai rien fait. J'avais trop la flemme.

was super sick.
étais grave malade.

I can't remember; I have a huge hangover.
Me souviens plus; j'ai une grosse gueule de bois.
The literal translation for hangover, *gueule de bois* is
"mouth of wood."

And, what're ya doin' tomorrow? Are you free?
Et, tu fais quoi demain? T'es libre?

Yeah sweetie, I'm off!
Ouais, ma belle, je bosse pas!

Yes, I'm free.
Oui, je suis dispo.

Nope, I'm working as usual.
Nan, je suis au taf comme d'hab.

No, I have things to do.
Non, j'ai des trucs à faire.

What do you like to do with your free time?
Qu'est-ce que t'aimes faire avec ton temps libre?

D'ya have any hobbies, babe?
T'as des hobbies, chérie?
Hobbies is the anglicized and commonly accepted form of *passe-temps.*

I'm totally into ... (for verbs or nouns)
J'adore...

Most def! I'm addicted to … (for nouns only)
Tout à fait! Je suis accro à …
In the expression *je suis accro à*, the noun and its definite article must agree. This would make it *au/à la/aux*. Example: *Je suis accro aux garçons* (I'm addicted to boys). This same rule applies to most à expressions.

antiquing.
chiner/aux brocantes.

biking.
faire du vélo/au vélo.

cooking.
faire la cuisine/à la cuisine.

dancing.
danser/à la danse.

drawing.
dessiner/au dessin.

working out.
faire du sport/au sport.

painting.
peindre/à la peinture.

partying.
faire la fête/à la fête.

playing the (guitar/piano).
jouer de la (guitare/du piano)/à la (guitare/au piano).

playing (basketball/soccer/tennis).
jouer à (au basket/au foot/au tennis).

reading.
lire/à la lecture.

doing yoga.
faire du yoga/au yoga.

Gossip LES RAGOTS

Secrets travel fast in Paris. As with anywhere, one can only talk about politics, current events, and pop culture for so long before it gets dull; gossiping is inevitable. From the daily grind, to romantic escapades, it's all fair game for a bitch sesh. However, just because cattiness sounds prettier *en français*, it's no reason to be nasty.

Darling, I'm DYING to know. How was your **date** last night?!
*Chouchou, je meurs d'envie de savoir. C'était comment ton **rancard** hier soir?!*

OMG it was incredible! He's a real …
Oh mon dieu c'était incroyable! Il est un vrai …

badass.
loubard.

charmer.
charmeur.

classy/cultured one.
mec classe/cultivé.

crack-up.
rigolo.

gentleman.
gentleman.

hottie.
canon.

smarty.
cerveau.

sweetheart.
amour.

Ugh, terrible. What a/an ...!
Pouah, terrible. Quel ... celui-là.

asshole
connard

bore
chieur

bum
clodo

cheeseball
ringard

horndog
chaud lapin

idiot
crétin

loser
loser

pain in the ass
casse-couilles
Literally, "ball-breaker."

player
coureur

smart-ass
petit malin

tight-wad
radin

Clara's been such a **bitch** lately … what's up with her?
*Clara a l'air d'une grosse **garce** récemment..qu'est-ce qu'elle a?*

She's got a shitload of **family issues**, poor baby.
*Elle a plein de **problèmes de famille**, la pauvre.*

Her boyfriend's fucking up her life.
Son copain lui salope la vie.
Note that the noun *salope* (whore/bitch) can be used as a verb meaning "to fuck up" or "to mess up."

She's failing all her **classes**.
*Elle rate tous ses **cours**.*

After her **all-nighters**, she's just beat.
*Après ses **nuits blanches**, elle est juste crevée.*

She just quit smoking.
Elle vient d'arrêter de fumer.

She got dumped.
Elle s'est fait plaquée.

I don't know, maybe she's just **PMSing**.
*Chais pas moi, peut-être qu'elle **va avoir ses règles**.*
The grammatically correct way to say "I don't know" is *je ne sais pas*, but the *ne* in negation is often dropped verbally and the whole expression is contracted.

You're kidding right? She's always like that!
Tu rigoles, elle est toujours comme ça!

Any news about Lou Lou? I miss her.
T'as des news de Lou Lou? Elle me manque.

Yes, she's really happy over there with her new life.
Oui, elle est très heureuse là-bas avec sa nouvelle vie.

Yeah, she doing super well!
Ouais, elle va super bien!

Last I heard she has a **new job**.
*La dernière chose que j'ai entendue c'est qu'elle a un **nouveau job**.*

Apparently she's super busy with **work**.
*On dit qu'elle est débordée de **travail**.*

She's obsessed with her new BF.
Elle est accro à son nouveau copain.

Nope, she stopped talking to me.
Nah, elle me parle plus.

Nothing at all.
Rien du tout.

Who cares? She pisses me off.
On s'en fout. Elle me gonfle / fait chier.
The expression to *faire chier* (literally, "to make shit") is very commonly used for someone/something that pisses one off. *Chiant(e)* is the adjective form for "annoying."

I couldn't care less.
Je m'en fiche/Je m'en balance.

I don't give a shit.
Je m'en fous.

Text Speak LES TEXTOS

Considering the literality of the French language, it comes as no surprise that *les Français* adore abbreviations. Rather than taking an hour to be a typographic pro, forget *à toute à l'heure* (see you soon) when you're texting, and just tap *à tt*. With all the tricky contractions and accents you've been wrapping your head around, give your pretty fingers a rest and ease off the clickfest. Yeah, you wanna know all the deets on who, what, where, when, and why, but here's a quicker way to get the subtext of that text. The less time you spend staring at the screen, the more time you have to scope the peeps you'll be sending 'em to.

Once you get a text, sounding out the symbol is your best bet to figure out what it means. Some general rules:

The number "1" replaces *un* and *une*, and the sounds *-en* and *-in*.

G1rv
j'ai un rendez-vous
 I have a date

The number "2" is used instead of *de*.

a2m1
 à demain
  see you tomorrow

The letter "c" is substituted for *c'est*, *sais*, *s'est*, and anything of that nature.

c cool!
 c'est cool!
  that's cool!

The letter "é" is used for the *ai*, *ais*, etc.

mé jé rien contre toi
mais je n'ai rien contre toi
 but I have nothing against you

The letter "k" can replace *qu* or *ca*. For example:

> *koi?*
> *quoi?*
> what?

The letter "o" can be used *for au, eau, aux.*

> *jél kado pr toi*
> *j'ai un cadeau pour toi*
> I have a gift for you

The letter "t" works for *t'es* and similar sounds.

> *TT où IR?*
> *T'étais où hier?*
> where were you yesterday?

And to articulate yourself:

INTRODUCTIONS

TEXT	VERBAL	TRANSLATION
bjr	*bonjour*	good morning
bj	*bonne journée*	have a good day
bsr	*bonsoir*	good-night
cv	*Ça va?*	What's up?
koi29?	*Quoi de neuf?*	What's new?
lut / Slt	*salut*	hey
savapas?	*Ça va pas?*	Is something wrong?

T4
❀

BASICS

TEXT	VERBAL	TRANSLATION
1	*un*	a
12c4	*un de ces quatre*	one of these days
2 ri1	*de rien*	you're welcome
c1blag	*c'est une blague*	it's a joke / JK
cad	*c'est à dire*	as in / i.e.
cb1	*c'est bien*	that's good
cpg	*c'est pas grave*	no big deal
entk	*en tout cas*	in any case
l's tomb	*laisse tomber*	forget it
mr6	*merci*	thanks / thx
o	*au*	at / in the
p2k	*pas de quoi*	it's nothing (you're welcome)
pdp	*pas de problème*	no problem
p-ê	*peut-être*	maybe
pk	*parce que*	because
qq	*quelques*	some
qqn	*quelqu'un*	someone
rdv	*rendez-vous*	date / appt.
stp / svp	*s'il te (vous) plait*	please
tt	*tout*	all / every
tps	*temps*	time / weather

EMOTIONS / STATES

TEXT	VERBAL	TRANSLATION
dsl	*désolé(e)*	I'm sorry
mdr	*mort de rire*	dead laughing / LOL
jsg	*je suis génial*	I'm great
jtm	*je t'aime*	I love you
raf	*rien à faire*	nothing to do

SUBJECT / VERB PHRASES

TEXT	VERBAL	TRANSLATION
c	*c'est*	it's / that's
ct	*c'était*	it was
g	*j'ai*	I have
GHT	*j'ai acheté*	I bought
gt	*j'étais*	I was
j	*je*	I
jc	*je sais*	I know
j'le sav	*je le savais*	I knew it
jv	*je vais*	I'm going
ss	*(je) suis*	I am
t	*t'es*	you are
TT	*t'étais*	you were
v1	*viens*	come
y a	*il y a*	there is / there are

INTERJECTIONS / QUESTIONS

TEXT	VERBAL	TRANSLATION
b1	bien	good
b1sur	bien sûr	of course
dacc	d'accord	ok
dc	donc	so
xlt	excellent	great
kan / kand?	Quand?	When?
keske?	Qu'est-ce que?	What?
ksk t'fu / kestufou?	*Qu'est-ce que tu fous?*	What the fuck are you up to?
ki?	*Qui?*	Who?
kl?	*Quel?*	Which (one)?
koi?	*Quoi?*	What?
pk?	*Pourquoi?*	Why?
re	*rebonjour*	hi again
TNRV?	*T'es énervé?*	Are you pissed?
TOQP	*T'es occupé?*	Are you busy?
vrMen	*vraiment*	really

DATE / TIME

TEXT	VERBAL	TRANSLATION
ap	*après*	after / afterward
auj	*aujourd'hui*	today
dm1	*demain*	tomorrow
dqp	*dès que possible*	ASAP
fds	*fin de semaine*	weekend
ir	*hier*	yesterday
mnt / now	*maintenant*	at the moment
tds	*toute de suite*	right away
we	*week-end*	weekend

SIGN OFFS

TEXT	VERBAL	TRANSLATION
a+	*à plus*	see you later
a2m1	*à demain*	see you tomorrow
AB	*à bientôt*	see you (someday) soon
ALP	*à la prochaine*	until next time
a tt	*à tout à l'heure*	see you (very) soon
biz	*bisous*	kisses / xx

Chapter 4

Culture: La Culture

"Whoever does not visit Paris regularly will never really be elegant."

—HONORÉ DE BALZAC, 1830

While it might be true that in France *la vie est belle* (life is beautiful), one can also say that it is *très cultivée*. As in, the French are a very cultured people. From Beauvoir to Godard to Voltaire, there's a whole alphabet soup of *Français* who have made their mark on contemporary society. Whether you're inside the Louvre marveling at 18th century masterpieces or meandering the streets admiring centuries' worth of architectural movements, cultural beauty abounds.

By simply fulfilling your role as an urban explorer, you're participating in an intellectual phenomenon. During the rebuilding of Paris in the 19th century, poet Charles Baudelaire popularized the notion of *le flâneur*, or "the stroller," who plays an integral part in the modern metropolis. By actively immersing yourself in your surroundings, you're not only stimulating your individual curiosities, but also being a figure in the overall aesthetics of the culture. Consider yourself a walking art form.

L'Art ART

Femininity has always been of high importance in the French art scene. While almost all the classic artists were men, their *égéries*, or muses, were just as important. Degas loved ballerinas, Toulouse-Lautrec adored the cabaret girls, and Matisse his blue nudes. Who's the girl that everybody's going paparazzi on in *le Louvre*? Mlle Mona Lisa, of course. Yes, *la Joconde* may be Italian by origin, but her enigmatic charm has made that museum one of the foremost in the world. Beyond the key collections there are countless specialty museums and galleries that are equally worth a visit. Even if museums aren't your thing, most artists today use the streets as their easels. Don't disregard the graffiti that surrounds you; those walls are an artistic movement in full bloom.

Check out the new **exhibit** that I told you about. You gotta see these ...
*Mate la nouvelle **expo** dont je t'ai parlé. Faut que tu voies ces ...*

> landscapes.
> *paysages.*
>
> mixed media.
> *œuvres mixed-media.*
>
> paintings.
> *peintures.*

photo(graph)s.
photo(graphie)s.

portraits.
portraits.

prints.
gravures.

sculptures.
sculptures.

sketches.
dessins.

textiles.
tissus.

I don't understand anything about … art.
Je comprends rien à l'art …

abstract
abstrait

conceptual
conceptuel

contemporary
contemporain

classical
classique

impressionist
impressionniste

modern
moderne

pop
le Pop Art

postmodern
postmoderne

What do you think of **the gallery opening**?
*Tu penses quoi du **vernissage**?*

It's cool.
C'est cool.

It's fucking crazy!
C'est un truc de malade!

It's whatever.
C'est kif-kif.

Its not my style.
C'ést pas mon trip.

I don't get it.
Je capte rien.

It sucks.
Ça craint.

Did you see that **graffiti**? That tagger's insane!
*T'as vu ce **graffiti**? Ce taggueur est ouf!*

Museums LES MUSÉES

While the Louvre may be the proud holder of some of the most renowned art on the globe, it is only one of the many museums worth your precious time in Paris. From anatomical oddities, to dolls, to postal history, all aspects of French life are on display for your intellectual expansion; be sure to *profiter* (take advantage). Likewise, museums often throw stellar special events, film screenings, and various lectures that make for great dates. Naturally you aren't the only girl that wants to get her art on. To avoid lines, arrive early, go on weekdays if possible, and buy your tickets in advance. Occasionally there are free days or student discounts, so keep that in mind too. While for some collections it might take a year to see it all, for others it takes just an hour. Regardless, every *arrondissement* has a museum or three, so there's no excuse to not set foot in one. Throw on your comfy heels and get cultured!

CENTRE GEORGES-POMPIDOU
place Georges-Pompidou, 4ème

Former President Georges Pompidou's namesake museum is an emporium of contemporary art. In contrast to the city's predominantly classic limestone architecture, this industrial structure is reminiscent of something you'd find in an

abandoned warehouse. If the building's paradoxical exterior isn't enticing enough, realize that behind all that colorfully "highlighted" piping is an inventive world of modern curiosities.

LA MAISON EUROPÉENNE DE LA PHOTOGRAPHIE
5-7, rue du Fourcy, 4ème

The European House of Photography showcases some of the foremost artists in contemporary photography. While photography is a deeply rooted fixture of French history, this museum showcases the work of photographers from all around the world. From Karl Lagerfeld's latest monochromatic campaign to an exposé on modern standards of beauty, this *Maison* always has a stylish appeal. Its exhibits spread out across five floors, so surely there is something that will strike your aesthetic fancy.

MUSÉE CARNAVALET
23, rue de Sévigné, 3ème

This 17th century mansion houses hundreds of years worth of Parisian history. A charming feature of the Marais, this free museum offers an engaging perspective of the past, with cultural mementos and *objets trouvés* (found objects) spanning the French Revolution to contemporary times. As you meander about the museum, take your time while marveling the period rooms, and get a taste of Parisian life across the eras. Feel free to visit the adjoining Hôtel Le Peletier de Saint-Fargeau, an archeological gem. The beautifully manicured courtyard gives a refreshing return to reality.

MUSÉE GALLIERA-MUSÉE DE LA MODE ET DU TEXTILE
10, avenue Pierre 1ere de Serbie, 16ème

After a long-awaited reopening, the newly renovated Fashion and Textile Museum brings the world of *mode* to a whole new level of intellect. Not only does it showcase costumes from the corseted days of Marie Antoinette, but an exposition on models throughout history or even fashion's relation to medieval art are on display as well. Treat the museum's halls as a cultural runway of sorts and strut your way through the exhibitions.

MUSÉE DU LOUVRE
99, rue de Rivioli, 1er

The museum that needs no introduction, the Louvre houses one of the most expansive and distinguished collections in the world. From the diminutive *Mona Lisa* to the soaring *Venus de Milo*, there are too many masterpieces to name among its 35,000-plus works. This former fortress has become its own circus with a food court and shopping mall underground in the *Carrousel*. Do not be overwhelmed by its grandiosity. Take in as much as possible in a day, and start early. Take a wing at a time, or simply follow the provided "must-see" guide; it's a shortcut to sophistication.

MUSÉE DE L'ORANGERIE
Jardin des Tuileries, 1er

Of the different museums found in the Tuileries Garden, this one is by far the most intimate. The former 19th century greenhouse was initially built for growing oranges, but since the 1920s it has solely housed the fruits of art. Of the various masterpieces that fill up this charming space, Claude Monet's *Nymphéas* are the true stars. Making you a subject in his personal pond, a large ovular room surrounds you with four of his breathtaking water lily paintings. If you can't make it to Monet's home in Giverny, the serene splendor of this room offers a nice Claudian repose from Parisian city life.

MUSÉE D'ORSAY
62, rue de Lille, 7ème

The glass-roofed museum that rests majestically along the left bank of the Seine was once a train station. Its belle époque architecture and imposing clock are as alluring as its renowned impressionist collection. The works span 1848–1914, so it makes a nice interlude between *le Louvre* and the various contemporary museums in the city. Though impressionism only accounts for a portion of the collection, if the names Cézanne,

87

Degas, Monet, or Renoir make your heart sing, this is the place to come.

MUSÉE DU QUAI BRANLY
37, quai Branly, 7ème

This state-of-the-art facility houses a garden, multimedia library, and troves of indigenous art. Its extensive collection of works from Africa, Asia, Oceania, and the Americas is presented in a thematic fashion spanning countless centuries. From high-tech displays to interactive exhibitions, this museum showcases a dialogue among ancient civilizations, with a modern twist. With original scriptures, costumes, cinema, artwork, and more, it offers a comprehensive view of the non-Western world and a delightful change from all the city's European-oriented museums.

MUSÉE RODIN
79, rue de la Varenne, 7ème

This museum pays homage to the work of sculptor Auguste Rodin. Including the renowned

piece *The Thinker*, whether placed in the stately mansion or outside along the backdrop of the garden, his bronze sculptures are both physically and artistically impressive. The museum not only comprises his sculpted works, but also photography, sketches, and various pieces he collected along the years, including works of Renoir and Van Gogh. Aside from the more classic art, occasionally there is a contemporary exhibit within the museum walls as well. You can visit the garden alone for 1€; pack a picnic lunch and enjoy. It's definitely worth the trip!

MUSÉE DE LA VIE ROMAN-TIQUE
16, rue Chaptal, 9ème

This charming Montmartre institution is indeed as picture-perfect as it sounds. Tucked away at the foot of a hill, this museum is devoted to evoking the days of the Romantic Era (1800–1850). Housed in Dutch painter Ary Scheffer's home, it is one of Paris's three literary museums, the Maison Victor Hugo and Maison Balzac being the others. The two-story pavilion displays mementos of novelist Georges Sand, as well as a host of Romantic portraits and memorabilia. Even if the exhibitions aren't of interest, the floral and fragrant courtyard is a lovely spot for a midday repose.

PALAIS DE TOKYO /MUSÉE DE L'ART MODERNE DE LA VILLE DE PARIS
13, Avenue du Président Wilson, 16ème

This extensive building hosts two museums, both dedicated to exhibiting contemporary art. The eastern wing has the city-owned Museum of Modern Art, and the western wing is the Palais de Tokyo. The Palais not only acts as an exhibition space, but also hosts a studio for artists in its pavilion. The museum is non-collection based, so the artists it exhibits are truly novel in their expression. During Fashion Week, *le Palais* is of interest not only due to the progressive exhibitions but also as the stage for several runway shows. For an inexpensive and thought-provoking look into the brightest minds of contemporary art, this dynamic museum does it all.

CHÂTEAU DE VERSAILLES
RER C to Versailles Rive-Gauche

While it may not be within the city limits, no trip to Paris is complete without popping into Versailles. One quick train ride and you'll be able to stroll about this palatial estate, with its ornate castle and gargantuan grounds. From the sparkly Hall of Mirrors to Marie Antoinette's personal palace, you will realize how French royalty had their cake and ate it too. The self-enclosed fantasyland is surrounded by a seemingly endless garden that is enjoyed by tourists and city natives alike. Lush fields, fountains, and daylong bike rentals make Versailles the perfect summer daytrip.

Cinema LE CINÉMA

France has a deeply rooted history in the world of *cinéma*.
Forget Hollywood, cinematography originated right here in
France under two brilliant and inventive brothers, Auguste
and Louis Lumière. Today, outside of the United States
and India, France is the globe's third-largest producer of
films, and walking around Paris will corroborate that in full.
From Hollywood blockbusters on *les Champs-Elysees* to
independent art-house flicks in *le Quartier Latin*, there
is something to see for everyone. While the nation might
not be as celeb-obsessed as America, the French get very
starstruck when a certain award ceremony rolls around. *Le
Festival de Cannes* is THE most anticipated entertainment
event of the year, and as tantalizing as the red carpet
is, having watched the films will make you all the more
embedded in the culture.

What's showing at the **movie theater** today? How 'bout ... ?
*Y a quoi au **ciné** aujourd'hui? Ça te dirait ... ?*

>   an action film
>   *un film d'action*
>
>   a chick-flick
>   *un film pour nanas*
>
>   a comedy
>   *une comédie*

a documentary
un documentaire

a drama
un drame

a dubbed film
un film en v.f. (version française)
Un film en v.o. (version originale) is in its original version
with subtitles.

a horror film
un film d'épouvante

an indie
un film indie

a rom-com
une comédie romantique

a sci-fi
une science-fiction

a western
un western

Let's go see that new (name of director or actor here) **film**.
*Allons voir le nouveau **film** de (nom du directeur ou acteur).*

Did you get **the tix**?
*T'as achêté **les billets**?*

I'm going to get some popcorn. **Do you want anything?**
*Je vais chercher des pop-corns. **Tu veux quelque chose?***

I'd love a **soda**.
*J'aimerais un **soda**.*

Where should we **sit**?
*Où est-ce qu'on devrait **s'asseoir**?*

There's a Godard retrospective at the Cinema Museum. I so admire his ...
Il y a une rétrospective Godard à la Cinématheque.
J'admire tellement son/sa/ses ...

> casting.
> *casting (m).*
>
> cinematography.
> *photo (f).*
>
> editing.
> *montage (m).*
>
> soundtrack.
> *bande sonore (f).*
>
> screenplays.
> *scénarios (pl).*
>
> plotline.
> *intrigue (m).*

What did you think of **the flick**?
*Tu pensais quoi **du film**?*

It was ...
C'était ...

all right.
pas mal.

awesome!
génial!

amazing!
incroyable!

crazy!
dingue!

soooo sick!
mortel!
Mortel can also mean "deathly boring" depending on your intonation.

hilarious!
trop marrant!

shitty!
de la merde.

What a stupid film!
Quel film débile!

It bored me to death!
Ça me barbait!

The book was better.
Le bouquin était meilleur.

Film-spiration CINÉ-SPIRATION

Being that French is such an aesthetically minded culture, nothing encapsulates *la Française* better than a lens, and you should take full advantage of that. Regardless if the story line is fictional or not, it will offer you a foretaste of the atmosphere, personalities, and lifestyle you might encounter in your daily life. Here are some titles and heroines of note, as well as several classic "*Américaines* in Paris."

A BOUT DE SOUFFLE BREATHLESS (1960)
Directed by Jean-Luc Godard
....

HEROINE: Jean Seberg
PLOTLINE: A charming petty criminal Michel is on the run in Paris with his American girlfriend Patricia. In typical Godardian fashion, this New Wave classic will challenge your moral, philosophical, and social standards, all in one aesthetically stunning package.
LE PARIS: A lot of cruising around the city, both leisurely and criminally. This era was all about shooting in the streets rather than on a set. Paris plays its own role in the film.

BELLE DE JOUR (1967)
Directed by Luis Buñuel
....

HEROINE: Catherine Deneuve
PLOTLINE: Séverine, a bored housewife, becomes a daytime prostitute in a high-class brothel. Under Spanish Surrealist Buñuel's direction, this film is a perplexing treat for the eyes and mind.
LE PARIS: A pretty depiction of the more uptown city culture. Yves Saint Laurent acted as costume designer, so the film's fashions are worthwhile on their own.

DREAMERS (2003)
Directed by Bernardo Bertulucci

HEROINE: Eva Green
PLOTLINE: Matthew, a young American student, comes to Paris, becomes a regular at *la Cinémathèque Française*, and befriends an overtly sensual sibling duo. The three become a *ménage-à-trois*, trying to isolate themselves from the student rebellions rampant outside their idealized world.
LE PARIS: A beautiful portrayal of the atmosphere of the tumultuous 1968 youth rebellion. While this film is full of HOT eye candy, it is a valuable homage to French cinema as well.

ET DIEU ...CRÉA LA FEMME AND GOD CREATED WOMAN (1956)
Directed by Roger Vadim

HEROINE: Brigitte Bardot
PLOTLINE: Bardot plays Juliette, a wayward orphan who flaunts her sexuality and seduces the (once sleepy) fisherman's village known as Saint Tropez.
LE PARIS: This film made both Bardot and Saint Tropez overnight stars. Her nymphet style and sex appeal encapsulate that quintessential *je ne sais quoi* of French women. You will see why she was *le cat's meow*.

FUNNY FACE (1957)
Directed by Stanley Donen

HEROINE: Audrey Hepburn
PLOTLINE: When a New York fashion magazine decides that the new "look" comprises beauty AND brains, they choose book clerk Jo Stockton to be cover girl. In true *Clueless* "project" fashion, they transform this scholarly gamine into a Parisian glamazon.
LE PARIS: Comical, musical depiction of both the fashion industry and beatnik café culture *à la parisienne*.

NIKITA (1990)
Directed by Luc Besson

HEROINE: Anne Parillaud
PLOTLINE: Nikita, a young junkie, gets caught in armed robbery and sent to prison. She's girlnapped and recruited by the government to be an assassin. She incarnates the modern femme fatale perfectly.

LE PARIS: Think Mrs. Smith meets Eliza Doolitle in the City of Lights. As Jean-Luc Godard once said, "All you need in film is a girl and a gun." And *voilà*, *Nikita*.

MARIE ANTOINETTE (2006)
Directed by Sofia Coppola

HEROINE: Kirsten Dunst
PLOTLINE: In all her extravagant splendor, we get intimate insight into the renowned and reviled Queen Marie Antoinette. This highly stylized film is both charming and saddening.
LE PARIS: Not much of Paris through Sofia Coppola's lens, but this gorgeous confection of a film relays the story of two essential parts of Parisian history: le Château de Versailles and its regal inhabitants.

PARIS, JE T'AIME
PARIS, I LOVE YOU (2006)
Directed by a different director per short, including the Coen brothers, Gus Van Sant, and Wes Craven

HEROINE: Many top actresses, including Catherine Deneuve, Juliette Binoche, Natalie Portman, Marianne Faithful, Maggie Gyllenhaal
PLOTLINE: Eighteen short films depicting the 20 arrondissements in Paris.
LE PARIS: From immigrant to native, boy to girl, younger to elder ... every type of Parisian tale is told in this dazzling anthology.

VIVRE SA VIE
TO LIVE HER LIFE (1962)
Directed by Jean-Luc Godard

HEROINE: Anna Karina
PLOTLINE: After countless failed attempts to become an actress, the charming 20-something Nana falls into prostitution. Her demise is Godard's commentary on femininity and sexuality in contemporary society.
LE PARIS: Filmed in 12 episodes, Godard shows life "on the streets" both in the figurative and literal senses. Real footage and outtakes depict the omnipresence of prostitution in the '60s Parisian scene.

Music LA MUSIQUE

While there might not be a particular genre of music that originated in France, the French have made their presence audibly heard over the years. In the early days, operas, ballets, and waltzes were solely a luxury for the wealthy. But in the cabaret era of the 19th century, music halls opened their boisterous doors to all, and a more popularized style of the *chanson française*, or French song, emerged. As pop music became all the more *à la mode*, the French girls made their mark with the mini-skirted melodies of the '60s *Yé-Yé* movement. Now most of the nation's music can be enjoyed while wandering the streets. From students banging *téchtronic* beats in Montparnasse to an accordionist playing a cheerful tune in Montmartre, Paris is an urban theater for your listening pleasure.

Did you get **the song** I sent you? I'm all about …
*T'as reçu **la chanson** que je t'ai envoyée? Je kiffe …*

> the beat.
> *le rythme.*
>
> the melody.
> *la mélodie.*
>
> the music video.
> *le clip.*
>
> the lyrics.
> *les paroles.*

the vocals.
la voix.

the whole album.
l'album entier.

The genre isn't really my thing. **I don't like ...**
Le genre n'est pas vraiment mon trip/truc. **J'aime pas ...**

Where can I go **to hear** ...?
*Où est-ce que je peux **écouter**..?*

blues
du blues

classical
de la musique classique

country
de la musique country

dubstep
du dubstep

electronic
de l'électro

folk
de la musique folk

hip-hop
du hip-hop

indie
de la musique indie (indépendante)

jazz
du jazz

punk
du punk

rap
du rap

rock
du rock

techno
de la techno

Yo, that's the new jam from Daft Punk!
Hé, c'est la nouvelle son de Daft Punk!

Crank it!
Monte le son!

Make it louder!
Mets la 'zique au fond!

That song's blowing up!
Cette chanson cartonne!

That's some good shit.
C'est du bon son ça.

It's SO overrated.
C'est grave surfait.

I can't stand it.
Je peux pas le supporter.

Turn that shit off!
Éteins cette merde!

Music Styles and Scenes
DES SCÈNES ET DES STYLES DE LA MUSIQUE

As Paris has a museum for everyone's aesthetic taste, it likewise has countless venues to satisfy any musical style. With certain locations, like the illustriously ornamented *Opéra-Garnier* or the infamous *Folies-Bergère*, it is rather obvious the type of show you will have in store. However, many a neighborhood resto-bar and street café transform into concert venues at night. Offering a wide range of live music, some will list the *agenda* or *programmation* (lineup) online while others you'll delightfully happen upon. Indulge yourself, twirl around, and please do bump into that cutie by the bar. If the scene gets old, simply take your new friend to the next spot and dance the night away. Here's a taste of what's in store if you're into ...

Classic French *(Chanson)*
Scene: While you may not be able to see these icons perform anymore, their voices have been revered on and off stage for decades. These stars began dazzling the hearts of café society during the Parisian Jazz Age (1920s) and continue to do so today.

Artists: Edith Piaf, Georges Brassens, Jacques Brel, Juliette Gréco

Electronic

Scene: The *Tecktonik* electro street style of dance originated in Paris, so electronic music has quite a French following. If the idea of moshing in line for a beat-heavy evening or getting down with DJs in an underground digital scene is prime, *voilà* your people.

Artists: Air, Daft Punk, Stèphane Pompagnac, Yelle

Hip Hop/Rap/R&B

Scene: You're hot, hip, and into hip-hop, or maybe the smooth and sultry R&B type. Wanna party hard and dance your ass off till daybreak? Let's find you a stylish sweatbox to meet some fellow scenesters.

Artists: Lady Laistee, Alpha Wann & Nekfeu, Booba, Youssoupha

Indie/Pop

Scene: Whether it be something mellow or a more upbeat pop band, you vibe with the indie set. One night might lead to a dance party in an abandoned warehouse along Canal Saint-Martin; another could be a chill sesh in Gambetta. Regardless, there is enough variety within the scene to give you a daily dose all of your indie cravings.

Artists: Autour de Lucie, Tryo, Miou Miou, Suarez

Jazz/Traditional

Scene: Dim lighting, wine by the bottle, and crooning tunes. For the nostalgic type who wants a throwback to the pre-digitalized days of song, Paris has many a speakeasy. Get drunk off the sweet sounds and charming ambience of the jazz scene, or simply reminisce on the cabaret days of yesteryear.

Artists: Django Reinhart, Émile Parisien, Josephine Baker, Michel Legrand

Punk Rock
Scene: How about a mix of class with a lot of sass in a red velvet den of debauchery? Indie bands and rock and roll are *de rigueur* and the attendees are of the pretty persuasion. In these gritty havens for the Parisian punk scene, beer might swing as freely as the bopping heads, so dress accordingly.

Artists: Guerilla Poubelle, Les Vielles Salopes, Noir Désir, Superbus

World
Scene: Paris is teeming with immigrants from all over the globe, so the possibilities are endless in terms of the world music scene. From African Zouk to Gypsy Jazz, the locals offer a lot to groove to. While the concerts are likely to be in a foreign-heavy hood like Belleville, both the artists and their followers break out of their comfort zones. This is, of course, the beauty of a multicultural sound.

Artists: Amadou et Mariam, Anges d'Afrik, Gypsy Kings, Orange Blossom

Vocal

Scene: The French *femme* is often considered to be aesthetically charming but with all the iconic songstresses it seems their musicality is just as seductive. These pretty ladies with their pretty voices will act as a lovely soundtrack to your Parisian escapades. Feel free to channel their killer styles as you do.

Artists: Brigitte Bardot, Charlotte Gainsbourg, Coralie Clément, Keren Ann

Chapter 5

Fashion: La Mode

"The Parisienne is not in fashion, she *is* fashion."

—ARSÈNE HOUSSAYE

Fashion is a way of life in France. Period. With many of the earliest design houses originating in Paris, *la mode* has always been a fixture in French history. Linguistically, think of its influence on the English language: mode, style, couture, and chic all come from *français*. Even the most American of fashions, denim, got its name from the city of Nîmes (*de Nîmes*). The biggest irony of the culture, however, is that being *à la mode* really has very little to do with being "in fashion."

Whereas some cultures obsess over what's "on trend" and adopting the latest "it" craze, the French have an innate style they embrace. The standard *Française* is building an investment wardrobe. Rather than having dozens of mediocre pieces, she has a dozen cherished items she thoughtfully purchased. Her wardrobe is a true reflection of herself.

There is no use trying to "emulate" the French style; it is more about an approach to clothing. Wear what you love and love what you wear. More importantly, love yourself in it. The sexiness of self-confidence with a sprinkling of *charm* and *élégance* is how you will channel your inner *Parisienne*.

Beauty LA BEAUTÉ

Something in the air seems to permit the French to coin the term "effortless chic," and there is an overwhelming sense of nonchalance in their beauty regimen. As such, the mussed hair, barely-there makeup, and overall "fuck it" vibe they exude might mystify someone who is used to a more "groomed" culture. Being unkempt is *de rigueur* in this city, but don't think you can simply let yourself go; it takes a little work to be so perfectly *au naturel*. The French art of *se soigner* (to take care of oneself) is more of an attitude change than a lifelong dependence on products. If you live well, eat well, and treat yourself with care, you will glow brighter than the *Tour Eiffel* and perhaps even pass for a *Française*.

I need a **makeover**.
*Il me faut un **relooking**.*

Where can I go to get ...?
Où puis-je faire faire...?

Let's go to the **beauty salon** to get ...
*On va au **salon de beauté** pour se faire faire ...*
When you have someone else do something for you, you say *faire* twice; when you do it yourself, only once.

> a facial
> *un soin du visage*

a manicure
une manucure

a pedicure
une pédicure

a (back/body/foot/Swedish) massage
un massage (du dos/intégral/des pieds/suédois)

a (bikini/eyebrow/leg/underarm) wax
une épilation à la cire (du maillot/des sourcils/des jambes/des aisselles)

our nails done
nos ongles

a blow-out
un brushing

a haircut
une coupe

highlights
un balayage

a rinse
un shampooing

Damn! I went through my makeup bag and I'm out of ...
Merde! J'ai fouillé ma trousse de maquillage et je n'ai plus de ...

Can I borrow your ...?
Je peux emprunter ton/ta ...? .

eye shadow
ombre à paupières (f)

eyeliner
eyeliner (m)

lip balm
baume à lèvres (m)

lipstick
rouge à lèvres (m)

makeup remover
démaquillant (m)

mascara
mascara (m)

moisturizer
crème hydratante (f)

nail file
lime à ongles (f)

nail polish
vernis à ongles (m)

nail polish remover
dissolvent (m)

perfume
parfum (m)

Pass me my toiletries. **I need** my …
*Passe-moi mes produits de toilette. **J'ai besoin de** mon/ma …*

comb.
peigne (m).

deodorant.
déodorant (m).

loofah.
loufa (m).

mirror.
miroir (m).

nail scissors. / nail clippers.
pince à ongles (f). / coupe-ongles (m).

razor.
rasoir (m).

tweezers.
pince fine (f).

Baby, I got a new **hairstyle.** Do you like it?
*Chéri, j'ai une nouvelle **coiffure**. Ça te plaît?*

It's adorable!
C'est adorable!

TOO CUTE!
TROP MIMI !
Mimi is short for *mignon.*

Fuck yeah! You look hot!
Putain, ouais! T'as l'air très sexy!

Obviously! I love the bangs.
Évidemment! Je kiffe les franges.

Honestly, no.
Franchement, non.

Not really.
Pas trop.

I hate it.
Je la déteste.

III

Clothing LES FRINGUES

The average person who is new to Paris will likely be underdressed. Both sexes make a discernible effort and this is what makes them so much hotter than the rest of us. You will find inspiration in many a *look* you see, but take note discreetly. *Les rues* are THE place to see and be seen so stay on you're A-game. Embrace your own style, but save any outlandish experimentation for your weekend trip to London. This is a culture where less is more, so chill out on the accessory/makeup/trend overload. Keep it simple and sassy and those perfectly rouged *Parisiennes* will drop jaw.

You see that girl over there? I'm DYING over her ...
Tu vois cette meuf là-bas? Je crève d'envie d'avoir son/sa/ses ...

Nice ...
Ton/Ta/Tes ____ est/sont super sympa(s)!

> bag
> *sac à main (m)*
>
> bling
> *bijoux bling-bling (mpl)*
>
> blouse
> *chemisier (m)*
>
> overcoat
> *manteau (m)*

dress
robe (f)

hat
chapeau (m)

jacket
veste (f)

jumpsuit
combinaison (f)

kicks
godasses (fpl)

overalls
salopette (f)

pants
pantalon (m)

tank
débardeur (m)

tee
tee-shirt (m)

top
haut (m)

shoes
chaussures (fpl)

shorts
short (m)

(mini)skirt
(mini)jupe (f)

style
style (m)

sweater
pull (m)

sweatshirt
sweat-shirt (m)

trenchcoat/raincoat
imper (m)
Imper is short for *imperméable*.

vest
gilet (m)

I'm so over my **wardrobe!** I need ...
*J'en ai marre de ma **garde-robe!** J'ai besoin de/d' ...*

a new look.
un nouveau look.

a new muse.
une nouvelle égérie.

some new **clothes**.
*des nouvelles **fringues/sapes**.*
Fringues and *sapes* are slang for *vêtements*. In a boutique you will only see *vêtements*.

114

a lot of **money**.
*beaucoup de **fric/de tunes***.
Argent is the formal word for "money."

I want some new **shoes**. Maybe some …
*Je veux des nouvelles **chaussures**. Peût-être des …*

lovely leather ballet **flats**.
*jolies **ballerines** en cuir.*

lace-up **ankle boots**.
***bottines** à lacets.*

blue suede **heels.**
***talons** en daim bleu.*

platform **sandals** for spring.
***sandales** à plateforme/sandales compensées pour le printemps.*

wellies for my trip to London.
***bottes de pluie** pour mon voyage à Londres.*

new Isabel Marant **sneakers**.
*nouveaux **baskets** d'Isabel Marant.*

And my **dress,** what do you think of it?
*Et ma **robe,** qu'est-ce que t'en penses?*

I like it.
Je l'aime.

I love it
Je la kiffe.

I really fucking love it!
Je la surkiffe!

I'm obsessed with it!
J'en suis obsédée! / J'en suis complètement accro!

That's super **"in"** right now.
*C'est super **tendance** en ce moment.*

You look so **hip**!
*T'as (Tu as) l'air grave **branchée**!*

It makes your ass look great.
Ça te fait un cul d'enfer.

It's too short, you look like a skank.
C'est trop court, ça fait pute.

For my **birthday** I'm treating myself to …
*Pour mon **anniversaire** je m'offre …*

a little black dress.
une petite robe noire.

some **skinny jeans** with ankle zippers.
*un **jean slim** avec des zips aux chevilles.*

a supersexy low-cut top.
un haut décolleté super sexy.

a rabbit fur coat.
un manteau en lapin.

I'm really into textures these days, especially ...
Je suis fan de la texture en ce moment, surtout ...

> fur.
> *de la fourrure.*
>
> knit (chunky/loose/fine).
> *de la maille (épaisse/grosse/fine).*
>
> lace.
> *de la dentelle.*
>
> leather.
> *du cuir.*
>
> silk.
> *de la soie.*
>
> suede.
> *du daim.*
>
> wool.
> *de la laine.*

I need some **accessories.** Where can I find some nice ... ?
*J'ai besoin d'**accessories.** Où trouve-t-on des ... sympas?*

I'm stocking up on ...
Je fais des réserves des ...

> beanies
> *bonnets*

117

belts
ceintures

bracelets
bracelets

chain bracelets
gourmettes

earrings
boucles d'oreilles

jewelry
bijoux

necklaces
colliers

rings
bagues

silk scarves
écharpes en soie

wide-brimmed hats
capelines

I need some new **lingerie**. I feel like *buying* ...
*J'ai besoin de nouvelle **lingerie**. J'ai envie d'acheter ...*

a bra (convertible/demi-cup/push-up/strapless/
triangle/wireless).
*un soutien-gorge (à bretelles amovibles/corbeille/
push up/bandeau/triangle/sans armatures).*

some undies (bikinis/boxers/boyshorts/G-strings/
thongs).
des slips (culottes/boxers/shortys/strings/tangas).

a bodysuit.
un body.

a camisole.
un caracos.

a garter belt.
un porte-jarretelles.

a nightgown.
une nuisette.

some pj's.
un pyjama.

a robe (cotton/fuzzy/satin).
*un déshabillé/un peignor (coton/toucher pelouche/
satin).*

some stockings.
des bas.

some tights (fishnet/footless/knit/opaque/printed/
plumetis/polka dot).
*des collants (résille/sans pied/maille/opaque/
imprimés/plumetis/à pois).*

High Fashion
LA HAUTE COUTURE

When people describe the City of Lights, you will often hear about its stylishness. A certain social aesthetic in Paris lends itself to be deemed the "fashion capital of the world." This is the product of decades of gorgeousness crafted by a handful of designers. While they might differ in style and era, there are discernible similarities in the French "look." Black, white, and a pop of color. This is the standard palette you'll see strutting about the city. Call it boring; call it classic; *c'est chic*. The monochromatic nature contrasts beautifully against the limestone backdrop of Paris, turning the streets into a runway of sorts. As Coco Chanel once said, "Fashion is in the sky, in the street ... the way we live, what is happening." It is indeed a part of *la vie parisienne*, and regardless if one shops at *H et M* or *Hermès*, all are well versed in high fashion. Here's a guide to get you schooled on style:

ALAÏA (1980)
7, rue de Moussy, 4ème

HISTOIRE (STORY): Famous for his severe feminine silhouettes, Azzedine Alaïa uses lingerie-fitting techniques, sculpting the body with cinched waists, super tight knit dresses and to-die-for (literally) platforms. A sartorial architect, his masterpieces are very expensive and *very* coveted. So coveted that Cher Horowitz was famously mugged while wearing this "totally important designer" in the '90s cult film *Clueless*.

FAMED FOR: Bodysuits, fetishistic heels, S & M couture
CURRENT DESIGNER: Azzedine Alaïa

BALENCIAGA (1918)
336, rue Saint-Honoré, 1er
....

HISTOIRE: Founded by Cristobal Balenciaga, this originally Spanish house opened shop in Paris in 1937, bringing the Basque culture to the French. In contrast to Chanel's androgyny and Dior's hourglass, Cristobal played with structure, proportions, and waistlines.
FAMED FOR: Motorcycle bags and leather jackets, opulent edginess, "it" pieces.
CURRENT DESIGNER (2012-): NY downtown denizen Alexander Wang replaced Nicolas Ghesquière after a 15-year stint. Ghesquière made Balenciaga a household name with his futuristic avant-garde designs, and now Wang's redefining Parisian monochrome with a bit of grit and a lot of glam.

CÉLINE (1945)
24, rue François 1er, 8ème
....

HISTOIRE: Céline Vipiana launched her label in 1945 and frankly left little legacy. A handful of faulty designers rotated until Phoebe Philo took the reigns in 2010 and drove the brand to become an indispensable industry staple. Every editor, every model, everybody wants a piece of Céline.
FAMED FOR: Stark luxe minimalism, luggage totes
CURRENT DESIGNER (2010-): Phoebe Philo took over Chloé in 1997, after former boss Stella McCartney started her own line, reviving it with the quintessential modern *bohème* look. In 2008 she took her Midas touch to Céline where she now has ladies drooling over her luxe leather goods and a sleek yet fierce ready-to-wear.

CHANEL (1909)
51, avenue Montaigne, 8ème
....

HISTOIRE: Mlle Gabrielle "Coco" Chanel made her mark during WWI when she liberated women from corseted torture and birthed the provocative yet practical drop-waist dresses of the Roaring Twenties. Coco wore pants, dated Nazis, and was an all-around rebel-rouser.

FAMED FOR: Little Black Dress (LBD), 2.55 handbag, wool suits, insignia embossing
CURRENT DESIGNER (1983–): Karl Lagerfeld is the infamous "Kaiser" of Fashion. Outside of Chanel, he designs for Fendi, as well as his eponymous collection. Likewise, from coke bottles to currency, he's put his face on just about everything in the market, including his own diet book. Lagerfeld has the most publicly recognized white ponytail since Washington.

DIOR (1946)
30, avenue Montaigne, 8ème

HISTOIRE: Christian Dior made waves with his debut collection, contrasting the austerity of post-WWII fashion with his feminine and extravagant "New Look." In opposition to the relaxed androgyny of Chanel, Dior redefined corseted silhouettes, giving women back the glam they were starved of during war rations. Hyper-femininity is a continued tradition *chez* Dior.
FAMED FOR: Full skirts, the "trapeze dress" (under YSL).

CURRENT DESIGNER (2012–): Raf Simons, the minimalist extraordinaire formerly at Jil Sander, replaced the theatrical John Galliano (after a very publicized snafu).

GIVENCHY (1952)
28, rue Saint-Honoré, 8ème

HISTOIRE: Hubert de Givenchy started his couture house with a ready-to-wear collection, full of modern and ladylike separates. His elegant simplicity made him loved by many, namely Jacqueline Kennedy and his longtime muse Audrey Hepburn. That infamous dress of his that she wore in *Breakfast at Tiffany's* put the LBD on the map.
FAMED FOR: Understated glamour, conceptual couture.
CURRENT DESIGNER (2005–): Riccardo Tisci has revitalized the house of Givenchy with architectural, sensual, and highly stylized designs. Collaborating with Kanyé West and Jay-Z on the Watch the Throne tour, he's earned much notoriety in hip-hop culture. Tisci's killing it with

his brilliant blend of prints, punk, and prettiness.

HERMÈS (1837)
24, rue du Faubourg Saint-Honoré, 8ème

HISTOIRE: Originally a saddlery in 1837, from 1880 on the Hermès family started designing womenswear, and over the course of the next century they introduced the zipper, their notorious silk scarf (*carré*), and a range of leather handbags that are still highly coveted pieces. Hermes has always had a notable clientele, including Princess of Monaco Grace Kelly and French icon Jane Birkin, both whom have bags named after them. That signature Hermès orange is as much of the French national fabric as blue, white, and red.
FAMED FOR: "Investment" bags, silkwear, equestrian chic.
CURRENT DESIGNER (2011–): Christophe Lemaire, plucked from Lacoste, continues the

equestrian influences of this classic French house.

ISABEL MARANT (1989)
16, rue de Charonne, 11ème

HISTOIRE: Isabel started out with accessories in 1989, alongside her hubby Jerome Dreyfuss, who has an eponymous accessories line as well. After introducing ready-to-wear in 1994 she has become the go-to girl for *la bohème*. With her slouchy separates, embellished jackets, and short flouncy dresses, she's a favorite among fashionistas worldwide.
FAMED FOR: Bohemian *à la parisienne*.
CURRENT DESIGNER: Isabel Marant

KENZO (1970)
60-62 rue de Rennes, 6ème

HISTOIRE: The Japanese designer Kenzo Takada started his line using fabrics he sourced from flea markets, resulting in a very eclectic and daring collection. The originality and miscellany of his designs were a refreshing departure from the standard neutral tones of Parisian fashions. His first boutique was called "Jungle Jap" and the inclination toward bold and animalistic prints has continued through today.

FAMED FOR: "Parisian Jungle."

CURRENT DESIGNERS (2012–): Humberto Leon and Caroline Lim. The dynamic duo behind the American lifestyle store/brand Opening Ceremony was recently appointed at the helm. Their logo prints, urban jungle themes, and a Vans collab have injected the formerly crumbling *maison* with a much needed dose of cool.

MAISON MARTIN MARGIELA (1989)
23/25 rue de Montpensier, 1er

HISTOIRE: This Belgian designer is revered for his avant-garde deconstructing tendencies. From wig coats to garbage bag jackets, Margiela turned ordinary objects into couture masterpieces. He has never shown his face in public and his clothes are equally anonymous. Only the four exposed white stitches outlining the white cloth label trademark a Margiela piece. The designer left the business some time ago, though the exact date of his departure was never confirmed.

FAMED FOR: Exposed seams, outlandish proportions, "anti-fashion."

CURRENT DESIGNER: A design team, as nobody could fill Margiela's enigmatic shoes.

RICK OWENS (1994)
130-133 Galerie de Valois, 1er

HISTOIRE: This fashion school dropout started working in the LA garment district knocking off designer wear, and these rebellious origins are perfectly synonymous with his aesthetic. He is American by birth, but French by design; his studio is currently based in Paris. Gothic grungy glamour is his forte and leather the material of choice.

FAMED FOR: Drapey leather pieces, funnel-necked black on black, sublime basics.

CURRENT DESIGNER: Rick Owens

YVES SAINT LAURENT (YSL) (1960)
53, avenue Montaigne, 8ème

HISTOIRE: After a brief stint at Dior, Yves Saint Laurent opened his own *maison* and popularized *prêt-à-porter* (ready-to-wear). The first couturier to truly democratize fashion, he ushered the Parisian "beatnik" look and drew inspiration from Oriental and African references. His villa in Marrakech, *le Jardin Majorelle*, is now a museum and testament to his lavish exoticism.

FAMED FOR: Safari chic, *le smoking* (female tuxedo), androgynous glamour.

CURRENT DESIGNER (2012-): Formerly at Dior Homme, Hedi Slimane, *a très* talented photographer/designer, is known for monochromatic heroin chic. In a rather controversial move, he dropped the "Yves" and retrograded the brand name back to *Saint Laurent Paris* (*SLP*).

Style LE STYLE

From Marie Antoinette to Carla Bruni-Sarkozy, France has had many a stylish icon at its helm to guide the people in its modish tendencies. However, fashion royalty aside, such an extravagant or conservative approach will not get you very far in your daily escapades. While it is never advised to limit oneself to a particular "aesthetic," with the multitude of different vogues in French history, you might find it helpful to have some references in defining *your* Parisian look. Do not think that the age-old Breton sweater, cigarette pant, ballet flat mix is a cultural standard. Nobody wears berets in Paris.

Here are some options to channel:

La Bohème

Channeling: You, my dear, long for the wayward bohemian ease of *les années 70*. The Marais is your playground and if you could, you'd take a goat vest over goat cheese any day. While you may not be able to caravan your way around the city, there are plenty of thrift shops that'll send you back in time.

Stydol: Jane Birkin, Françoise Hardy

Uniform: Minidress, floppy hat, Mary Janes, woven bag. Lace top and wide-leg jeans.

Boutique: Free "P" Star, Hippie Market

Magazine: *Please!, Mirage*

Blog: misspandora.fr, leblogdelamechante.fr

La Bombe

Channeling: As the glamourpuss that makes both *les garçons* and *les filles* purr, you have no qualms about soaking up all the sensuality in the *parisien* air. Sure you strut your stuff down *les Champs-Élysées*, but you equally enjoy a "personality" *pâtisserie* at Ladurée. You've been pining for some vintage Dior since you popped out of the womb, and if you're a good girl you'll get some.

Stydol: Brigitte Bardot, Catherine Deneuve

Uniform: Leopard coat, little black dress, fuck-me heels, cat eye sunglasses

Boutique: Pretty Box, Bastien de Almeida

Magazine: *Vogue Paris*

Blog: byglam.fr, absolutelyglamorous.fr

La Branchée

Channeling: You hip, hot thang. After following all the street style blogs for years, you're finally being snapped yourself. Models off-duty are your muses and leather anything your vice. Doesn't matter if you're young, broke, and fabulous or just plain fabulous, you run this town like a boss.

Stydol: Aymeline Valade, Emmanuelle Alt

Uniform: Leather jacket, white tee, skinny jeans, combat boots, "it" bag, heavy bling

Boutique: Colette, L'Imprimerie

Magazine: *Self Service*, *Purple*, *Numéro*

Blog: le-21eme.com, l-echappee-belle.tumblr.com

La Gamine

Channeling: You may not be the "it" bitch or even the sexiest chick in the room, but you've got charm for days. A modern darling sitting at a café reading a book or being read to by the boy next to you, as sweet as a *macaron*. Regardless if it's an androgynous day or a girly one, you're unconventional beauty makes you the quintessential *Parisienne*.

Stydol: Audrey Tautou, Jean Seaberg

Uniform: Wool/trench coat, sweater, stovepipes, ballet flats. Little frocks for frolicking.

Boutique: Maison Kitsuné, Merci

Magazine: *So' Chic*

Blog: garancedore.com, leblogdebetty.com

Shopping LE SHOPPING

While meandering the beautiful city streets, you'll notice how easy it is to drain your savings on the regular. Paris is rife with boutiques, and you will be tempted to shop *all the time*. However, in true native fashion, you must *faire du lèche-vitrine* (window shop). Literally translated, the culture wants you to "lick the windows." Ogle every frill of that gorgeous dress you see, but do not feel obligated to purchase. Surely there will be something just like it, it if not better, around the corner. Likewise, you'll be overwhelmed by the fabulous *filles* sashaying about, and want to befriend them all and learn their secrets. The French aren't as open to spontaneous flattery as we are; don't gush over her hair, dress, and aura simultaneously. However, an honest-and-humble compliment might just point you to an otherwise insider's-only gem.

Hey Sophie, I'm about to max out my credit card …
Hé Sophie, je suis au point d'exploser ma carte bleue …

at a boutique!
dans une boutique!

at Chanel!
chez Chanel!

at the department stores!
aux grands magasins!

at the flea market!
au marché aux puces!

at the jewelry store!
à la bijouterie!

at the store!
au magase (magasin)!

at the thrift store!
à la friperie!

at the sales!
aux soldes!

on the Balenciaga bag in the window!
sur le sac Balenciaga dans la vitrine!

Excuse me, Ma'am, **I'm looking for** ...
*Excusez-moi, Madame, **je cherche** ...*

Where is/are ... ?
Où est/sont ...

the fitting rooms
les cabines d'essayage

the price of this skirt. **How much is it?**
le prix *de cette jupe.* ***Ça coute combien?***

the register
la caisse

the sale rack
les articles soldés

the women's department
le rayon femme

I love ...
J'adore ...

I'm not feeling ...
Je sens pas trop ...

the cut.
le coupe.

the color.
la couleur.

the fabric.
le tissu.

that brand.
cette marque-là.

the print.
l'imprimé.

the collar/neckline (cowl/high/round/V).
le col (roulé/montant/rond/V).

sleeves.
les manches.

Hayoo, that's ...
Ooh là, c'est ...

perfect!
parfait!

so dope!
trop frais!

my size!
ma taille!

on sale!
soldé!

super expensive! It costs an arm and a leg!
hyper cher. Ça coute la peau des fesses.
Literally, "It costs the skin off your ass."

Shit, it's really ...
Merde, c'est hyper ...

big.
grand.

long.
long.

loose.
lâche.

short.
court.

small.
petit.

tight.
serré.

ugly.
moche (cheum in verlan).

Size TAILLE

What is your size?
C'est quoi ta taille?

What is your shoe size?
C'est quoi ta pointure?

I wear a ...
Je porte une taille ... (clothing)
Je chausse du ... (shoes)

Do you have this in a/an ...?
Est-ce que vous avez ça en ...?

> extra small
> *XS*
> *You say your clothing size in letter form.*

> small
> *S*

> medium
> *M*

> large
> *L*

> extra-large
> *XL*

> the next size up
> *la taille au-dessus*

> the next size down
> *la taille en-dessous*

Size conversions:

CLOTHING							
US size	**XXS**	**XS**	**S**	**M**	**L**	**XL**	**XXL**
FR Women	34	36	38	40	42	44	46
FR Men	44	46	48	50	52	54	56

SHOES								
US size	**5**	**6**	**7**	**8**	**9**	**10**	**11**	**12**
FR Women	36	37	38	39	40	41	42	43
FR Men		39	40	41	42	43	44	45

Shops LES MAGASES

There is many a store type in Paris. From century-old flea markets to cutting-edge concept shops, the city has something for all tastes and more importantly, all budgets. Naturally, many a book has been written about each genre of boutique, and they offer a comprehensive directory to 20 *arrondissements'* worth of spending possibilities. While the serious shopper should consult said guides, here's a little snapshot of your new divine yet dangerous playgrounds. Proceed with caution ...

BOOKSHOP / *LA LIBRAIRIE*

TRANSLATION: All the artistic and written gems this culture capital can offer. Shakespeare & Co is a renowned American bookstore and has a bit of a cult following. Ofr. is a fashionista's literary paradise.

WHO THEY'RE FOR: Aesthetes, bookworms, students.
WHAT YOU'LL FIND: Textual and visual fodder, magazines, great gifts, and maybe a dinner date.
PRICE RANGE: €–€€
TOP 4: Artazart, Ofr., Page 189, Shakespeare & Company

CONCEPT SHOP / *LA BOUTIQUE CONCEPT*
....

TRANSLATION: Emporiums of chic with an emphasis on unknown labels, high design, and hip fashions. Concept shops are stores where a particular "concept" serves as foundation for the store. They are selling a lifestyle. Often double up as galleries/party throwers/cafés/etc. Colette is often called the world's dopest boutique. There's a water bar in the basement, and the windows are a treat in themselves.

WHO THEY'RE FOR: Those with deep pockets and an eye for style. Or the young, broke, and fabulous who stay in the know.

WHAT YOU'LL FIND: Cool shit. Techie toys, offbeat products, scenesters, celebs.

PRICE RANGE: €€€

TOP 4: Colette, L'éclaireur, Merci, French Trotters

CHAIN STORES/*DES CHAÎNES (DES MAGASINS)*
....

TRANSLATION: Upscale shops that can be found littered around the city. Naturally H et M, Zara, Mango, and all the other European retailers are omnipresent, but these are smaller specialty boutiques.

WHO THEY'RE FOR: Those who will neither skimp on quality nor drain their travel fund to stay *en vogue*.

WHAT YOU'LL FIND: Looks inspired straight from the runway of medium-grade and at midrange prices.

PRICE RANGE: €€

TOP 4: Maje, Sandro, Iro, The Kooples

DEPARTMENT STORES / *LES GRANDS MAGASINS*
....

TRANSLATION: Take the American style multifloored multi-department epicenters and put it in a lavish architectural masterpiece. That would be commercialism *à la parisienne*. *Le Bon Marché* was one of the world's first department stores, and *les grands magasins* have been dazzling both shoppers and sightseers for decades.

WHO THEY'RE FOR: Everyone, especially tourists.

WHAT YOU'LL FIND: Everything.

PRICE RANGE: €–€€€

TOP 4: Galerie Lafayette, Le Bon Marché, Printemps, BHV

FLEA MARKET / *LE MARCHÉ AUX PUCES*
....

TRANSLATION: Endless rows of miscellaneous goods for shoppers to meander through leisurely. The four largest markets are on the outskirts of the city but smaller *marchés* can be found daily throughout Paris.
WHO THEY'RE FOR: Collectors, bargain-hunters, thrill-seekers, and the curious.
WHAT YOU'LL FIND: From rare antiques to 1-euro clothing bins, there's something to tantalize everyone's palate here.
PRICE RANGE: €–€€€
TOP 4: Marché ...d'Aligre, Clignagncourt, Montreuil, Porte de Vanves

THRIFT STORE / *LA FRIPERIE*
....

TRANSLATION: Secondhand clothes piled together from questionable sources. These places are marvelous to stock up on unique "Oh, I got this in Paris" items without breaking the bank.

WHO THEY'RE FOR: Patient clotheshorses.
WHAT YOU'LL FIND: Lush furs, leather boots, granny sweaters, cheap dresses, and silk scarves galore.
PRICE RANGE: €
TOP 4: Free 'P' Star, Guerrisol, Hippy Market, Noir Kennedy

VINTAGE SHOP / *LA BOUTIQUE VINTAGE*
....

TRANSLATION: Upscale designer and antique fashions that are well curated and well taken care of. Not the chaotic forage of a thrift store, but you pay for the luxurious experience as well. Many of these shops are globally renowned, so a celeb spotting would not be unheard of.
WHO THEY'RE FOR: Fashionistas, history buffs, daydreamers.
WHAT YOU'LL FIND: Investment pieces, a gorgeous blast from the past, that Chanel 2.55 you've wanted since birth.
PRICE RANGE: €€–€€€
TOP 5: Yukiko Paris, Didier Ludot, Pretty Box, Réciproque

Chapter 6

Cuisine: La Cuisine

"In France, cooking is a serious art form and a national sport."

—JULIA CHILD

Whether it be a restaurant with a Michelin star or a chef who studied at Le Cordon Bleu, the French stamp of approval always means gastronomic goodness. Even our modern "American Nouveau" (New American) cuisine Frenchified itself to symbolize a refinement of the classics. It's been said that France reigns supreme in the richness of their cuisine. Imagine a world so intoxicating that it excites all of your senses without even trying. A land where you step outside your door and the inviting smell of freshly made bread taunts you as you pass a window filled with perfect pastries. Your sugar high won't last very long, however, the cheese shop down the street will tantalize an entirely different palate. This epicurean paradise exists, and it's called Paris. The ovens here are definitely magical, and everything is baked better *à la française*. Perhaps the chefs have some Midas touch, or it's simply their devotion to spreading happiness with butter. Whatever they're doing, it's damn good, and they'll show you food in a whole new light. The City of Lights, that is.

Behaving at the Table
BIEN SE TENIR À TABLE

In France there is a whole cultural credo on dining. Considering that they're more formal in even the simplest of introductions, naturally the French have elevated dining decorum. Obviously if you're at *le Macdo* (McDonalds), you can eat with ease, but even at a casual brasserie there are some general principles to follow. Breaking any of the rules will not only distinguish you as a foreigner but might also offend those whose company you are in. Now, darling, don't get so stressed you lose your appetite; simply be mindful of your manners. Regardless, whether you're in a restaurant or in the comfort of *chez toi*, France is not a fast food nation, so slow down *à table* (at the table). Savor every bite, you little *gourmande*. *Bon appétit!*

Breakfast
Le petit déj' / petit déjeuner
Unlike the American notion of breakfast being the most important meal of the day, in Paris it is the smallest. The standard way to start your day is with a coffee, a croissant or tartine (a split piece of baguette), and butter/jam. For the Frenchiest, this will also include *la clope du matin* (the morning cig).

Lunch
Le déjeuner
If you're looking for a lunch special, check the *ardoise* (slate board of specials) outside restos for the *formule* or *menu*. These *prix-*

149

fixe (fixed-price) options might include a *boisson + plat + dessert* special. This would be a drink, a main course, and dessert. Yeah that's right, having dessert with lunch is the norm, but you can skip it if you prefer. While you can sit down and have *une salade*, it's equally common to hit up a bakery and grab a sandwich on the go.

Late afternoon snack
Le goûter / Quatre-heures

While *le goûter* typically exists for children post-school around 16h, it is important to know that the French don't snack as we do. This little treat typically consists of a drink and/or a sweet. Even for those of us who are used to having multiple smaller meals spread out across the day, the French are rather strict in their three-meal allowance. *L'happy hour* is widely celebrated from 17h (5 p.m.) on as in the States, and the coffee-cig combo is acceptable 24/7, but note how these are both liquid encouragements. Basically they amass a lot of hunger for their most important meal of the day ...

Dinner
Le dîner

While the tradition of an epically elongated dinner has changed a lot, the other meals are smaller in comparison because dinner used to be a nightlong affair. In a very formal setting you could have countless courses: *l'amuse-bouche* (bite-size starter); *l'apéro/l'apéritif* (cocktail); *l'entrée* (appetizer); *le poisson* (fish); *le plat principal* (main course); *la salade*; *du fromage* (a cheese plate); *le dessert*; and *un café* (a coffee) or *un digestif* (post-dinner drink). But a main course, salad, and dessert are most common. The obligatory bread basket and wine will most likely go along with that. A more modern family or person may just have a main and then nibble on some cheese or dessert as desired. When entertaining, or when at the home of the more old-school bourgeoisie, people might have more courses. For the most progressive types, Picard's frozen goods have mastered the art of non-time-consuming French classics.

At a restaurant AU RESTO

While there isn't a single block in the city that isn't littered with restaurants, some *arrondissements* are more varied in their selection than others. For standard French fare, any corner bistro should do. However, an authentically international array can be found in an immigrant-heavy hood like Canal Saint-Martin or Belleville. Noshing *à la française* doesn't necessarily mean an expensive affair, but it will be a delightful one. There's a cultural pride in French gastronomy, and even the simplest of restos will try to leave you with a lasting impression. From chocolates with your *café* to personalized flatware, the experience is as much about prettiness as it is your palate. Between the specials and the classics, you might find the menu at a fancier resto a bit daunting, but you can also experiment with *un ménu-dégustation* (tasting menu) and get multiple dishes in teenier portions. The type of restaurant you choose will also denote the type of etiquette you must maintain. Show your best manners *à table* and charm your way right through that three-course meal. Dabble in the delicacies and try something new; your *escargots* won't bite, promise.

Darling, where are we going for ...?
Chéri(e), on va où pour le ...?

> breakfast
> *petit-déj(euner)*
>
> brunch
> *brunch*
>
> lunch
> *déjeuner*
>
> dinner
> *dîner*
> Both *déjeuner* and *dîner* can be used as verbs as well, for
> example: *Allons-y, on déjeune/dîne.* (C'mon, we're having
> lunch/dinner.)
>
> snack
> *goûter*
> *Goûter* as a verb means "to taste."

Have you eaten yet?
T'as mangé déjà?

Ugh, I'm so thirsty. I want a ...
Pouah, j'ai trop soif. J'ai envie d'un/une ...

> beer.
> *bière (f).*
>
> cocktail.
> *cocktail (m).*

coffee.
café (m).

coke.
coca (m).

juice (grapefruit/orange/pineapple).
jus (de pamplemousse/d'orange/d'ananas) (m).

lemonade.
citron pressé (m).

soda.
soda (m).

tea.
thé (m).

tea (herbal).
tisane (f).
You might be offered *une tisane* when at someone's home
after a meal, especially in the evening.

(red/rosé/white) wine.
du vin (rouge/rosé/blanc) (m).

(still/sparkling) water.
de l'eau (plate/gazeuse) (f).

I'm a little hungry. C'mon, let's go eat.
J'ai un petit creux. Allez, on va bouffer.
Bouffer is slang for the formal *manger* (to eat).

Ooh my, I'm starving. Let's hit up a restaurant.
Ooh là je crève la dalle. On se tape un resto.

Waiter/Waitress
Serveur/Serveuse

Here is the **menu**.
*Voici la **carte**.*

Our **specials** of the day/of the evening are ...
***Nos plats** du jour/du soir sont ...*
Most commonly, *plats du jour* are served in the evening too.

What would you like?
Que désireriez-vous?

What are you having?
Que prenez-vous?

What would you like to order? **To drink? To eat?**
*Que voudriez-vous commander? **À boire? À manger?***

Have you decided?
Vous avez choisi?

Yes. I would like ...
Oui. Je voudrais/j'aimerais ...

No, not yet. Another minute please.
Non, pas encore. Une minute, s'il vous plaît.

Can you tell me what you would recommend for a ...
Qu'est-ce que vous recommanderiez comme je suis ...
Literally, "Tell me what would you recommend as I am ..."

diabetic?
diabétique?

vegetarian?
végétarien(ne)?

vegan?
végétalien(ne)?

I don't eat ... (fish/meat/gluten)
Je ne mange pas de ... (poisson/viande/gluten)

Excuse me, Madam, we're missing a ...
Excusez-moi, Madame, il nous manque un/une ...

fork.
fourchette (f).

knife.
couteau (m).

spoon.
cuillère (f).

napkin.
serviette (f).

plate.
assiette (f).

setting.
couvert (m).

Is everything okay?
Tout se passe bien?

Yum! Everything's absolutely delicious.
Miam! Tout est absolument délicieux.

Yes! My steak is perfectly …
Oui! Mon steak est parfaitment …

>   well-done.
>   *bien-cuit.*
>
>   medium-rare.
>   *a point.*
>
>   rare.
>   *saigant.*
>
>   very rare.
>   *bleu.*

Yes, we ate very well. I'm full.
Oui, on a très bien mangé. J'ai plus faim.
Although the literal translation for "I'm full" is *je suis pleine*, it also means "I'm pregnant," so say this instead.

It was a real treat.
C'était un vrai régale.

Unfortunately, no. My meal is a bit too …
Malheureusement, non. Mon repas est un peu trop …

>   bitter.
>   *amer.*

cold.
froid.

hot.
chaud.

raw.
cru.

salty.
salé.

spicy.
épicé.

stale.
rassis.
As in stale bread.

sweet.
sucré.

overdone.
cuit.

The check, please.
L'addition, *s'il vous plaît.*

Restaurant Rules
Les Règles au Restaurant

Bread is basically sacred and will be served with any soup/salad/entrée (that doesn't already come on bread) you order. If for some reason it isn't, don't hesitate to inquire: *Du pain, s'il vous plaît.* (Some bread, please.)

Water, on the other hand, is not offered unless you specify. If you ask for water, they will bring you a shiny glass bottle of Evian and charge you for it. Tap water, *l'eau du robinet,* is free, but be sure the server hears you on that request. You can also ask for *une carafe d'eau* if you want a bottle of tap.

In terms of tipping, just as taxes are included in a price tag, generally the tip is included as well. If your *addition* (bill) says *service compris* (tip included), then you don't have to worry about a thing. If it doesn't mention, or your waiter says otherwise, all you need to leave is 10-15%. Whereas the American standard has become 18-20%, it is not as high in France.

House Manners
Les Bonnes Manières à la Maison

When you're *chez* someone, due to the intimate setting and personal relationship, your manners are all the more important. The French are classically very private when it comes to their homes, so don't be surprised if you aren't invited to the kitchen and are solely shown the living/dining room (and obviously the bathroom). Bringing a bottle of wine or a box of chocolates is always appreciated. If it's *à la fortune du pot,* or a potluck, bring something yummy, but otherwise don't offer. Again, in a more formal setting, assume the chef has it covered. However, if you're among your young, broke, and fabulous friends, bringing something'd be mighty nice!

Feel free to season what someone has prepared for you; everyone has their own *goût* (taste) and your host would rather you enjoy it than not. That being said, put on your best poker face if you really do dislike the meal, and try as much as possible to eat everything. It is seen as rude to leave too much on your plate.

Another note: you'll find your bread directly on the table (unless there's a bread plate). Whereas for us there's nothing wrong with biting off a piece of bread and nibbling throughout the meal, that's an absolute *non-non* in France; use your fingers to rip off a piece instead. For crusts and cheese rinds: if your host has left them on, leave them be and deal. It can be seen as rude to cut 'em off, so use your best judgement.

Grocery Shopping À L'ÉPICERIE

Though reality might quell your dreams of dining at every table the city has to offer, there are many alternatives to eating out. Going to the *supermarché* (supermarket), cooking *chez toi,* or "bringing your own" to a nearby park are all delightful ways to keep both your wallet and your appetite full during your Parisian stay. Realize that the French norm of grocery shopping isn't a "one-stop" approach, though *Monoprix* and *Franprix* exist as the

French equivalents to an American supermarket. Each food group has its very own specialty shop, and the cultural philosophy is that it's better go connoisseur when it comes to *la cuisine*. This means that as soon as you've finished hotfooting around the city to nab the perfect dress for your dinner party, you've got a whole 'nother bout of shops for the ingredients themselves. At least this shopping isn't as dangerous, unless of course you're more tempted by cheese than couture!

I'm going to the local ...
Je vais ... du coin.

> bakery.
> *à la boulange(rie)*

> butcher shop.
> *à la boucherie/charcuterie*

> candy store.
> *à la confiserie*

> cheese shop.
> *à la fromagerie*

> dairy shop.
> *à la crémerie/laiterie*

> farmer's market.
> *au marché*

> fish shop.
> *à la poissonnerie*

produce store.
au magasin de fruits et légumes

grocery store.
à l'épicerie

supermarket/giant superstore.
au supermarché/hypermarché

wine shop.
chez le marchand de vins

Food LA NOURRITURE

French cuisine has been long revered for its orgasmic-ness, and there's a logical reason for that. The fundamental ingredients of French cooking are butter, cream, eggs, and flour. Meat, cheese, and potatoes make the cut too. Basically, take any combination of those things and you've got yourself some traditional French fare: *des crêpes, des omelettes, du gratin, des soufflés,* etc. They are very yummy yes, but rather calorically laden too. Where are the fruits and veggies you ask? They're hiding in your *tartes,* my dear. Obviously you'll be able to find a salad on the menu—probably with goat cheese toasts on top, but don't expect a host of low-cal options at the *brasserie.* Vegetarianism is a recently accepted concept, so don't be surprised if some Frenchies think that includes *le poulet* (chicken). Regardless, you won't plump up overnight; the secret is moderation. There's no need to indulge in every pretty pastry you see in the window; there'll be another *pâtisserie* right around the corner. Treat yourself often, but don't eat yourself silly.

Baking Goods / *Ingrédients pour les Desserts (Les Gâteux)*

flour
farine (f)

nuts
noix (fpl)/fruits secs (mpl)

sugar
sucre (m)

Condiments and Seasonings / *Condiments et Assaisonnements*

garlic
ail (m)

jam
confiture (f)

mayonnaise
mayonnaise (f)

mustard
moutarde (f)

pepper
poivre (m)

salt
sel (m)

vinegar
vinaigre (m)

Dairy / *Produits Laitiers*

butter
beurre (m)

cheese
fromage (m)

milk
lait (m)

yogurt
yaourt (m)

Desserts / *Desserts*

cake
gâteau (m)

candy
bonbons (mpl)

chocolate
chocolat (m)

cookie
biscuit (m)

ice cream
glace (f)

Fruits / *Fruits*

apple
pomme (f)

lemon
citron (m)

lime
citron vert (m)

pear
poire (f)

raspberry
framboise (f)

strawberry
fraise (f)

Grains / *Céréales*

bread
pain (m)

pasta
pâtes (fpl)

rice
riz (m)

Meat, Protein / *Viande, Protein*

beef
bœuf (m)

chicken
poulet (m)

duck
canard (m)

eggs
œuf(s) (m)

fish
poisson (m)

ham (raw/smoked/boiled)
jambon (cru/fumé/blanc) (m)

lamb
agneau (m)

pork
porc (m)

(smoked) salmon
saumon (fumé) (m)

sausage
saucisse (f)

seafood
fruits de mer (mpl)

shrimp
crevettes (fpl)

Vegetables / *Légumes*

bean
haricot (m)

carrot
carotte (f)

lettuce
laitue (f)

mushroom
champignon (m)

onion
oignon (m)

potato
pomme de terre (f)

spinach
épinards (mpl)

tomato (sun-dried)
tomate (séchée) (f)

To the kitchen! EN CUISINE!

While you may not have a French maid costume handy,
nothing is more fun than getting your culinary chic on.
Host a dinner party for your new friends, bake your crush
a little something special, or simply treat your newfound
Parisian fabulosity. Or, if scouring gingham blankets for
Parisian babes is your jam, then bring your wine 'n' cheese
to *la Place des Vosges*. A homemade picnic is an equally
lovely way to toast a beautiful summer day *à la française*.
Just as you're expanding your cultural horizons, experiment
with some unusual combos and broaden your eating
horizons too. Likewise, bring some of your favorite dishes
from home and share them with your favorite Frenchies.
Remember they use the metric system, so factor that into
any homegrown recipes you use. Pop on that *tablier* (apron)
and get cooking, girlfriend!

Cooking Implements and Utensils
Les Ustensiles de Cuisine

bowl
un bol, un saladier

can
une boîte (de conserves)

cup
une tasse

dash
un filet

frying pan
une poêle

heat (low/medium/
high)
*du feu (petit/moyen/
grand)*

measuring cup
*un verre mesureur/un
verre gradué*

pan
une casserole/une cocotte

oven
un four

stovetop
une cuisinière

tablespoon
une cuillère (c.) à soupe

teaspoon
une cuillière (c.) à café

Preparations
Les Préparations

baked
cuit au four

boiled
bouilli / cuit à l'eau

diced
coupé en dés

dried
séché

fresh/chilled
frais (m)/fraîche (f)

fried
frit

grilled
grillé

puréed
écrasé/en purée

sliced
coupé en tranches/rondelles
Tranches are for breads, cakes, and meat. *Rondelles* are for
carrots, onions, sausage, and other round things.

skewered
en brochette

steamed
à la vapeur

stuffed
farci

Recipes RECETTES

Soup: French Onion Soup
La soupe: Soupe à l'oignon classique

Centuries ago this classic entrée was once only for the
poor, because onions were bountiful, but now it has
become much more popularized. There's even a national
tradition around this warm and odorous dish. To top
off New Year's Day, many restaurants will serve *soupe à
l'oignon* as the "first soup of the year," giving Frenchies a
cultural way to recover from a heavy dose of partying.

6 SERVINGS (POUR 6 PERSONNES)

> 5 medium yellow onions (*oignons moyens*), peeled and finely sliced
>
> 3 shallots (*échalottes grises*), finely minced
>
> 3 garlic cloves (*gousses d'ail*), finely minced
>
> 3 tbsp olive oil/butter (*huile d'olive/beurre*)
>
> ½ cup red or white wine (*vin rouge ou blanc*) (optional/*facultatif*)
>
> 4 cups beef, chicken, or vegetable stock (*bouillon de boeuf, de pouletou, de légumes*)
>
> thyme (*thym*)
>
> salt and pepper (*sel et poivre*)
>
> 6 slices of bread (*pain*), 1-inch thick
>
> 2 cups grated gruyère/emmenthal cheese (*fromage rapé*), or a blend

In a large pot at low heat, sauté the onions, shallots, and garlic in the butter/oil, and stir often until they're blinging gold, about 15 minutes.

Douse with the wine and add the stock and the seasonings. Salt and pepper to your liking. Bring it to a boil over high heat, then reduce the heat and let simmer for about 20 minutes.

Preheat the oven to 400ºF (200ºC).

Toast the bread on a baking sheet in the oven. Remove the bread then turn the oven up to broil.

163

Pour the soup into 6 ovenproof bowls. Place a slice of grilled bread in each and cover with 1/3 cup of cheese. Broil them while floating on top of the soup and serve.

Main course: Tuna and ratatouille with herb salad
Le plat principal: Thon à la ratatouille et salade d'herbes fraîches

In addition to the standard bistro fare, another popular French culinary style is "Provençale," which hails from the sunny southern Provence. There is more of a Mediterranean influence, so the recipes favor oils, herbs, and fish rather than the butter and flour-laden, meaty French basics. As such, it's a "lighter" fare. Ratatouille is the staple vegetable dish of this cuisine, so for you veggies out there, feel free to omit the fish. Let the richness of this provincial classic transport you to a gastronomic paradise, and imagine being along the lovely Riviera.

4 SERVINGS (POUR 4 PERSONNES)

> 1 zucchini *(courgette)*
> 1 eggplant *(aubergine)*
> 4 peeled tomatoes *(tomates pelées)*
> 1 red pepper *(poivron)*
> 1 big onion *(gros oignon)*
> 2 garlic cloves *(gousses d'ail)*
> olive oil *(huile d'olive)*
> 1 glass dry white wine *(verre de vin blanc sec)*
> 1 sprig thyme *(thym)*

salt and pepper *(sel et poivre)*
2 thick slices tuna *(tranches de thon)*
flour *(farine)*

HERB SALAD
4 eggs *(oeufs)*
basil *(basilic)*, parsley *(persil)*, chives *(ciboulette)*,
and any lettuces you'd like *(feuilles de laitue
mélangées)*
black olives *(olives noires)*
capers *(câpres)*
olive oil *(huile d'olive)*
balsamic vinegar *(vinaigre balsamique)*
Salt *(sel)*

Ratatouille: Wash and cut the vegetables: the zucchini
and eggplant in slices, the tomatoes into quarters, and the
pepper into strips. Dice the onion and the garlic.

Heat the oil in a large saucepan, and toss in the mixed garlic
and onions. Add the vegetables and stir in with the wine.

Season as you please. Let simmer on low heat for 45
minutes.

Salt and pepper the tuna slices. Roll in flour and cook in a
pan in hot oil. Flip them over after 2–3 minutes. Leave a few
more minutes until cooked to your taste.

Transfer the ratatouille to a plate and place the tuna slices
on top.

Salad: Hard-boil the eggs, and slice. Mix all the salad ingredients and serve with the ratatouille. Congratulate yourself on your healthy meal and toast it with a massive dessert.

Dessert: Blueberry almond clafoutis
Le dessert: Clafoutis aux myrtilles et aux amandes

··

The classic clafoutis is a sweet flan made with cherries, though you can substitute with any fruits, nuts, or even make it savory with cheese and veggies. This delightful dessert is light, simple, and most importantly suuuper good—it has never disappointed.

6 TO 8 SERVINGS (POUR 6 À 8 PERSONNES)

> 1 cup (5 oz) blueberries *(myrtilles)*
>
> 1 cup fruity wine *(vin)* such as Reisling or Muscato (optional/*facultatif*)
>
> 5 tbsp butter *(beurre)* plus more for buttering the baking pan
>
> 4 large eggs *(œufs)*
>
> ½ cup granulated sugar *(sucre en poudre)*
>
> ½ cup flour *(farine)*
>
> 1 cup whole milk *(lait entier)*
>
> 1 tbsp vanilla *(extrait de vanille)*
>
> ½ cup sliced almonds *(amandes éfilées)*

Preheat the oven to 325ºF (160ºC) and butter a shallow 2-qt. baking dish. In a small bowl, soak the blueberries in the wine for about 15 minutes, if using.

Melt the butter. In a large bowl whisk the eggs and sugar together. Add the flour until well mixed and gradually whisk in the milk, melted butter, vanilla, and remaining wine from the fruit bowl. Mix until smooth liquid concoction. Drain the blueberries or drink the fruit wine as you please and transfer the fruit to the baking dish. Scatter the blueberries and the almonds (save some nuts to sprinkle on top later if you'd like) on the bottom of the dish. Don't bother arranging them prettily; unfortunately, prebaked, this treat looks like clafoutis soup. Pour the batter carefully in the dish and watch your blueberries and almonds swim to the top.

Bake on the upper third rack of your oven (or on the only rack if you've a petite Parisian kitchen) until the dessert is puffed up, 45-60 minutes. When you let it cool, the puffiness will set; this is desired (not like a soufflé).

Dust with almonds, powdered sugar, or nothing at all. Serve the clafoutis warm or chilled. Feel free to add ice cream or whipped cream if you're feeling especially devilish. Savor every bite!

Chapter 7

Love: L'Amour

"I like Frenchmen very much because even when they insult you
they do it so nicely."

—JOSEPHINE BAKER

So you've been really good about taking in the culture in all its aesthetic, edible, and historical glory, but babygirl, *let's get physical.* It's about time you nabbed yourself some good French lovin' regardless if it be a full-blown relationship or just a one-night affair. Paris is often coined the "City of Love" as romance seems to always be in the air and romancing comes quite naturally. You'll rarely be hard-pressed to find a companion for the evening as the French are much less sexually conservative than the average American. Now, conventional dating can also be in your future obvi, but realize that the French mentality is a bit different from ours. The whole "bases" system of having certain steps that lead from one to the other is rather laughable to them. It can come down to this bed or be wed ideology, with not much gray area in between; they'll shower you with affection *and* attention for one night only or forever. Don't take these matters too seriously, unless of course you want to. Just hop on that Parisian love train and enjoy the ride!

Flirting LA DRAGUE

Along with cooking and caféing, flirting is visibly a national pastime. It can be as innocent as the baker at your *boulangerie* who gives you a wink while ringing up your *baguette* or some skeezball trying to get in your hot pants at a bar. The point is *la séduction* is second nature in this culture, so be considerate yet careful in how you respond. Occasionally we American girls play along with someone out of sheer courtesy so they don't feel bad, but in France keep all playfulness for someone you genuinely like. If you seem the slightest bit into it, they might take all your *non-non-nons* (nos) to be *oui-oui-ouis* (yeses). Be upfront in your rejection. But for the ones that aren't total creeps, bat them lashes, babe, and sprinkle in some of that American charm. They'll eat you up like candy.

I wanna ....
J'ai envie de ...

> **hit on** some (guys/girls).
> ***draguer*** des *(mecs/meufs).*

> get laid (by a guy/girl).
> *me taper (un mec/une meuf).*

> **have a quickie** in the bathroom.
> ***tirer un coup rapidos*** *aux chiottes.*

Yo, the girl sitting next to you is ...
Hé, la meuf assise à côté de toi ...

checking you out.
te mate.

crushing on you.
a flashé sur toi.

Look at that **cutie** over there.
*Mate cette **bombe** (f, whether the person in question is male or female) là-bas.*

D'ya think I should I ask for his/her **number**?
*Tu crois que je devrais lui demander son **numéro**?*

Go talk to him/her!
Vas-y, parle-lui!

I'm too shy.
Je suis trop timide.

He's totally into you.
Il craque pour toi.

See that guy over there? By the end of tonight I'm gonna ...
Tu vois le mec là bas? Avant la fin de la soirée je vais ...

>   buy him a drink.
>   *lui offrir une verre.*
>
>   chat him up.
>   *le brancher.*
>
>   dance with him.
>   *danser avec lui.*
>
>   get his digits.
>   *avoir son numéro.*
>
>   kiss him.
>   *l'embrasser.*
>
>   go home with him.
>   *rentrer avec lui.*

172

Pick-up Lines
PHRASES DE DRAGUE

It should come as no surprise that *les Français* are natural-born charmers. You could be picked up as easily at a boutique as at a bar. But any Frenchie with the slightest chic will avoid pick-up lines and use a more old-school approach. However, at a sketchy club or walking home on the streets you're bound to hear lots of *eeeh maademoiselles*. He might follow you a bit; he's from a determined breed. It's second nature for the French to covet something they find beautiful, especially if it's walking right in front of them. Overall he means no harm, so just put him in his place. Here's how to shut 'em down with style and success.

Classic Lines

Did it hurt when you fell from the sky?
Est-ce que t'as eu mal quand t'es tombée du ciel?

> No, it hurt when you opened your mouth.
> *Nan, j'ai eu mal quand t'as ouvert ta gueule.*

You must be tired because you've been running through my head all day.
Tu dois être fatiguée parce que t'as trotté dans ma tête toute la journée.

> Actually, I'm tired because you're boring me.
> *En fait, je suis fatiguée parce que tu me gonfles.*

173

Disgusting

Hey, nice rack!
Tiens, y a du monde sur le balcon!
Literally, "There are a lot of people on the balcony."

> Yeah, I hope you fall off.
> *Ouais, j'espère que tu en tombes.*

Wow, what gorgeous legs! What time do they open?
Waouw, jolies jambes! À quelle heure elles ouvrent?

> For you, they're permanently closed.
> *Pour toi, elles sont définitivement fermées.*

And if he really can't take a hint ...

I'm not interested. Good-bye.
Tu m'intéresses pas. Bye.

Leave me alone!
Laisse-moi tranquille!

Go away!
Casse-toi!

Get off me!
Dégage! Laisse-moi!

Shut up!
Ta gueule!

Shut the fuck up!
Ferme ta clape-merde!

174

Fuck off!
Fous le camp!

Go fuck yourself!
Va te faire foutre!

Dating SORTIR

Darling, if you're workin' that American beauty right, you should catch a Parisian's eye in no time. The French, romantic as they are, love some good ol' fashioned wooing. Whether you're the object of affection or vice versa, be subtle in your seduction. Cafés are the perfect spots for *rendez-vous* as you can make a quick exit after one coffee or linger for hours and lap up *du vin* (some wine). Or, perhaps get cozy at an exhibition that interests you both and have an intimate discussion afterward. The beauty of Paris is that almost any locale provides the perfect setting for a date, with lovely restos for snacking and darling benches for macking. Perhaps let them gauge what their intentions are for you. But if all goes well between you two, doll, you'll be exploring a lot more than just the city.

So this guy **asked me out** yesterday. He was really ...
*Alors un mec **m'a invitée à sortir** hier. Il était vraiment ...*

That girl is ...
Cette meuf est ...

> beautiful *(m/f)*.
> *beau/belle.*

175

buff / built.
baraqué / bien foutue.

cool.
branché(e).

cute.
mignon(ne).

hot *(m/f).*
une gravure de mode/bandant(e).

sexy.
sexy.

tall.
grand(e).

Ugh, my **blind date** last night sucked. This guy/girl was super ...
*Pouah, mon **blind-date** hier soir craignait. Le mec/La meuf était super ...*

dirty.
sale.

fat.
gros(se).

lewd.
vulgos.

nasty.
vilain(e).

skinny.
maigre.

short.
petit(e).

ugly.
moche.

He/She stood me up.
Il/Elle m'a posé un lapin.
Literally, "He left me a rabbit."

He/She asked me what I wanted to do for our first **date.** I was thinking …
*Il/Elle m'a démandé ce que je voulais faire pour notre premier **rancard**. Je pensais à …*

dinner and a movie.
un dîner et un film.

dancing.
une soirée en boîte.

a gallery opening.
un vernissage.

Louise's party.
la soirée de Louise.

a picnic.
un pique-nique.

a walk in the park.
une balade au parc.

What do we do together? Well, lately we spend a lot of time ...
Qu'est-ce qu'on fait ensemble? Bon, récemment on passe beaucoup de temps à ...

cooking.
faire la cuisine.

fighting.
se disputer.

going out.
sortir.

reading.
lire.

staying in.
rester à la maison.

watching movies.
regarder des films.

We'd been dating for a few months but we broke up. He/ She became too ...
On est sorti ensemble pendant quelques mois mais on a rompu. Il/Elle devenait trop ...

annoying.
chiant(e).

controlling.
directif/directive.

demanding.
exigeant(e).

distant.
distant(e).

full of shit.
complètement faux cul.

lazy.
fainéant(e).

possessive.
possessif/possessive.

selfish.
égoïste.

I miss my ex. He/She was really …
Mon ex me manque. Il/Elle était vraiment …

fun.
marrant(e).

hot.
sexy.

nice.
sympa.

perfect.
parfait(e).

sweet.
gentil(le).

Yeah, my ex was such a/an …
Ouais, mon ex était un tel …

asshole/bastard.
connard (m)/connasse (f).

dickhead.
con.
This is the figurative "jerk" version. The body part is *une bite*, with dozens of other translations. The word's female version, *conne,* is both the insult and physical "cunt."

jerk.
enfoiré(e).

loser.
loser.

In the Bedroom
DANS LA CHAMBRE

Frenchiness and fornication go hand in hand. Unlike America where sensuality can often be a social taboo, in France they're very open when it comes to sex, literally.

Talking dirty is so much sexier *en français*. Don't stress if you find yourself in Paris not falling in love and not finding a boy/girlfriend per se. Slip into something slinky and let's get your kitty *miaou-ing!*

Foreplay *Les préliminaires*

I love it when we ...
J'adore quand on ...

I get so hot when you ...
Ça m'excite quand tu ...

Does it turn you on when I ...?
Ça t'allume quand je ...?

> French kiss
> *(je te, on se) roule (tu me) roules des pelles*
>
> massage (my/your) back
> *je te masse, tu me masses, on se masse le dos*
>
> talk dirty
> *(je, tu) dis, (on se) dit des cochonneries*

What's your fantasy?
C'est quoi ton fantasme?

Got any fetishes?
T'as des fétiches?

Body parts *Les parties du corps*

Be gentle with my ...
Vas-y doucement avec ...

Caress my ...
Caresse ...

Tickle my ...
Chatouille ...

> breasts.
> *mes seins / mes nichons (a little naughtier).*

> booty.
> *mon cul.*

> ears.
> *mes oreilles.*

> hips.
> *mes hanches.*

> lips.
> *mes lèvres.*

lady bits.
chatte / minou.

Literally, "cat/kitten." I know the word "pussy" doesn't have the nicest connotation in English, but in French culture it's perfectly acceptable. They would even say "I get my puss waxed monthly" in casual convo.

Doin' the dirty *Faire des trucs cochons*

I wanna ...
Je veux ...

> make love.
> *faire l'amour.*

> be on top.
> *être dessus.*

> have a quickie.
> *tirer un coup rapidos.*

You're really turning me on.
Tu m'excites grave là.

Do you have a rubber?
T'as une capote?

Are you on the pill?
Tu prends la pillule?

Do you like it like that?
Tu l'aimes comme ça?

Mmm. That feels really good.
Mmmm. C'est vraiment bon ça.

I really like that!
J'aime beaucoup ça!

Don't stop!
N'arrête pas!

Do it ... / I want it ...
Fais-le ... / Je le veux ...

      again.
      encore.

      deeper.
      plus profond.

      faster.
      plus vite.

      slower.
      moins vite.

      harder.
      plus fort.

      softer.
      moins fort.

I'm about to cum.
Je vais jouir.

I'm coming!
Je jouis!

That was incredible. Wanna do it again?
C'était vraiment bon ça. On se le refait?

Chapter 8

Nightlife: La Vie Nocturne

"In Paris, our lives are one masked ball."

—GASTON LEROUX

You know those terrible moments when you're all dressed up with nowhere to go? Well in Paris, every place is worthy of your finest, and the possibilities are endless. Just as the streets are runways of sorts, wherever you might find yourself *en soirée* (out for the evening) is fitting to see and be seen. This is not to say that every spot is a guaranteed snobfest (as Parisian myth might have it), but rather any occasion is worthy of a more sophisticated self. Whether you have an intimate gathering at a friend's apartment, enjoy a lovely dinner *au bistro,* or simply want to chill at a café for hours on end, there are many ways to have a luxuriously laid-back evening. On the contrary, if you wanna put your heels to work on the dance floor, you definitely have that option too! Yeah, the last train leaves at 1:30 a.m. on the weekends, *and?* A true Parisian partier will simply wait for *le premier métro* (first metro of the day at 5:30 a.m.). Whatever you end up doing, babe, keep it *chic* and you're bound to have some French fun!

Going out SORTIR

The best thing about Parisian nightlife is that it's full of surprises. You might think you're being a good girl having a lil' post-dinner drink, until you look at your watch and suddenly it's 3 a.m. Turns out the bar you thought was merely for drinks is actually a dance club after hours. No, you weren't imagining those beats bumping beneath your feet. This seemingly innocent café might just have a mysterious door that opens up and leads you downstairs to a leather-walled sweatbox. Get real friendly with *le barman* (bartender) and hopefully you'll stay nice and "hydrated" till the wee hours *du matin* (of the morning). The trick to getting in is all about discretion. Look *damn* good and play yourself up as a *Parisienne*; keep all drunken American outbursts to a minimum. Don't roll up 15 people deep, as girls are always preferred over guys. Note that despite Paris's night-loving culture, the last train (*dernier métro*) leaves the terminal station at 12:30 a.m. on weekdays and 1:30 a.m. on weekends, resuming at 5:30 in the morning, so factor that into your party plan. And if you're working your "cab-to-curb" heels, taxis run 24/7 but aren't nearly as prevalent as in NYC; have one on speed dial or find a taxi station. Regardless, if you hit a bar or a colossal club, be prepared for a bout of spontaneity: Ya never know how it'll start off, or who you'll go home with!

Hey babe! D'ya have any **plans** tonight? I'm bored shitless.
*Salut chérie! T'as des **projets/plans** ce soir? Je me fais trop chier.*

Me too. I'm down for anything!
Moi aussi. Je suis prête à tout.

Good. Let's party.
Bon. Faisons la fête!

C'mon we're going out.
Allez, on sort!

Let's go to a club and pull an all nighter!
On va faire la fête en boîte toute la nuit!

I wanna **have a good time**, but I'm going home early.
*Je veux **m'éclater** ce soir, mais je vais rentrer tôt.*

I'm totally beat. I think I'll just ...
Je suis crevée. Je pense que j'vais ...

> go home.
> *rentrer.*

> stay in and watch a movie.
> *rester à la maison et mater un film.*

> go to sleep early.
> *me coucher tôt.*

> catch up with you guys tomorrow.
> *vous rattraper demain.*

189

Stefan told me about this new __. Let's check it out!
Stefan m'a parlé d'un nouv(eau/elle) __ . On va le mater!

>   after-party
>   *after (m)*
>   In this case it would be, "*un nouvel after.*"
>
>   bar
>   *bar (m)*
>
>   bar-restaurant
>   *resto-bar (m)*
>
>   club
>   *boîte (de nuit) (f)*
>   While you can dance and drink in most hip cafés/bars in
>   Paris, the standard "club" is a totally different affair. They
>   can be found in a wealthy/touristy area (i.e., Champs/
>   Montparnasse), and they're huge, charge covers, and draw
>   a somewhat skeezy crowd. It's a Euro thing and worth a try
>   but not the best for a laid-back or chill evening. Great for
>   sloppy dance floor make-out seshes though!
>
>   gallery
>   *galerie (f)*
>
>   music bar
>   *café-concert (m)*
>   Reminiscent of a jazz club, live background music, cabaret,
>   French folk, etc. Occasionally there will be a cover, but it
>   might also be a "weekly special" that the café does on the
>   regular.

party
soirée (f)

wine bar
bar à vins (m)

191

What do you think of the **club**?
*Tu penses quoi de la **boîte**?*

It's banging here!
Ça chauffe ici!

It's a hot mess.
C'est un bordel.
Literally, "a brothel."

Killin' it!
Ça déchire!

Not bad.
Pas mal.

It sucks.
C'est nul.

It's sketch as fuck.
Putain, ça craint grave.

What a dump!
Quel trou!

Should we ... ?
On ... ?

dance
danse

go
bouge

get outta here
se tire / se casse

I'm leaving. D'ya wanna .... at **the apartment** with me?
*J'y vais. Tu veux ... à **l'appart** avec moi?*

chill
glander

hang
traîner

crash
pioncer

sleep over
passer la nuit

Hoods QUARTIERS

So you're all luscious, lipsticked, and ready to go, but *où est la fête?!* (where's the party at?!) Well that depends, gorgeous, what are you in the mood for? Perhaps a little red wine pre-game along the banks of *la Seine* followed by clubbing on *les Champs*? A secret soirée at the newest *point-chaud* (hotspot) your new *copine* told you about in Pigalle? In Paris the possibilities are endless, and each *quartier* can hold its own. Let's see what your night has in store!

Tonight I wanna ...
Ce soir je veux ...

Ball out *Flamber, tout claquer*
Les Champs-Élysées 8ème

See all those flashing lights outside the crowded door on the Champs? That red carpet is rolled out and no, it's not a movie premier, it's a giant club, sweetie, and a world of moneyed *mecs* and naughty *nanas* awaits. If crazy covers and VIP areas aren't your scene, head to one of the intimate hotel bars or überchic hotspots in the area. Hidden among the dazzling storefronts lie their designer clientele sipping €24 cocktails. Surround yourself with *du beau monde* (the beautiful people) and smile pretty, darling, it's raining euros!

What is the **cover charge**?
*C'est combien **l'entrée**?*

Is there a **dress code** there?
*Y a un **code vestimentaire**?*

I want to go to the club with the **flashing lights**!
*Je veux aller à la boite avec les **lumières clignotantes**!*

You've gotta be **loaded** to get in there!
*Tu dois être **pété(e) de tunes** pour y entrer.*

Oh, that's just for **VIPs**.
*Oh, c'est que pour des **VIPs**.*
Another common term is "des people," pronounced "pee-pole."

Dine, drink, & dance *Dîner, boire, et danser*

Canal Saint-Martin 10ème

So you're strolling along the Canal mesmerized by how beautifully lit up *la nuit* is and you look around and realize the secret to its charm. The neighboring bistros and resto-bars are full of liveliness, and yet the serenity of the water gives the mood a special glow. Hence all the night crawlers romancing along its border. It's a lovely spot to split a bottle on a restaurant terrace and hear street performers jamming in the background. Cue the magic; here you'll find those picture-perfect moments you came to Paris for.

Can we have a table outside, please?
Est-ce qu'on peut être assis dehors, s'il vous plaît?

Let's order **a bottle of** wine.
*Commandons **une bouteille de** vin.*

What a nice view!
Quelle vue!

What instrument is that **street performer** playing?
*De quel instrument joue **l'artiste de rue**?*

Let's find **a spot** where we can dance!
*Trouvons **un endroit** où on peut danser!*

195

✾

Get down 'n' dirty *Mettre le feu*
Faubourg Saint-Denis 2/10ème

This hood is home to underground clubs. Not just because they're so cool you've gotta be an insider to know about 'em but also because you'll actually have to go underground to get your dance on. They might say it's "members only" or that it's a "private party," but if you play your cards right and look the part (i.e., straight off a fashion blog), you'll strut right in. Otherwise, you can always make nice with the hottie smoking outside and start your own party. It's worth the effort—ya never know what'll go down at these dens of debauchery.

Shake it, girl!
Meuf, bouge-toi!

Let's find a spot to stash our purses and hit **the dance floor**.
*Planquons nos sacs et fonçons sur **la piste de danse**.*

Do you see **that hottie** over there by the bar?
*Tu vois **cette bombe (m/f)** là-bas à côté du bar?*

Go dance with him/her.
Vas-y, danse avec lui/elle.

Cheap thrills *Des frissons à bas prix*

Le Quartier Latin 5ème

By daylight *le Quartier Latin* might seem like nothing short of an academic playground for the university students of *La Sorbonne*, but at night it's an entirely different scene. Those bookworms turn to babes and come out of the libraries to play. Bars with the student budget in mind are sprawling across the neighborhood. Full of inexpensive shots, well drinks, and beer galore, they're like fraternities *à la française*. What better way to break the ice with the cutie by the bar than doing Jell-O shots off their bod?!

Let's go barhopping!
Faisons la tournée des bars!

Where can we find the cheapest tequila shots around here?
Où est-ce qu'on peut trouver *les shots de tequila les moins chers dans le coin?*

What are we **celebrating**?
*Qu'est-ce qu'on **fête**?*

I hope you don't have **class** tomorrow morning!
*J'espère que t'as pas **cours** demain matin!*

Chill out and be cool
Être tranquille
(Haut) Marais 3/4ème

Swanky bars and cute cafés that stay open late abound in
le Marais. Surely you've noticed the hood exudes insane
hipness during the day, and, darling, it's twice as good at
night. If you hit the same spot where you had your mid-
shopping treat, you'll find *les* girls have slipped out of their
thrifted ensembles and into somethin' slinkier. This is the
heart of gay Paris, sweetie. The neighborhood isn't prime for
dancing your ass off, but it's a great way to warm up or cool
down.

Let's hit up that restaurant we went to for lunch the other
day.
Faisons le resto où on a déjeuné l'autre jour.

Cool and cultured *Cool et cultivée*
Pigalle 9ème/18ème

If your ideal evening starts at a gallery opening, gets going at
a bar, and ends grooving till dawn, this is the place for you.
Intellectuals, artists, and partiers alike flock to the nighttime
hotspots sprinkled about the area. One evening might be a
book club gathering and another a fashion event—that's just
how they roll *à Pigalle*. From bars to dance halls to sitting
on the steps of *Le Sacré Cœur*, there are plenty of spots to
have your mind expanded.

Are there any more galleries around here?
Y a d'autres galeries dans le coin?

I've had enough art. Let's head to the bar down the street.
J'en ai marre de l'art. Allons au bar plus loin dans la rue.

Rock out *Se dechaîner*

Bastille 11ème

Very different from the neighboring Marais, *Bastille*'s
appeal is in its slightly hidden and gritty club scene. Varied
indie, punk, and rock music will lure you from one place
to another, and cheap drinks will keep you going all night
long. It could be fun or downright filthy, but you can be
sure that you'll be effectively intoxicated, if not by your own
liquid doing perhaps by the spiky sexpot at the door or the
charmer behind the mike seducing you with his lyrical steez.
If all goes the way you have it planned, you'll have some
backstage adventures too!

This is a sweet show!
Ce spectacle est génial!

I can't hear anything you're saying!
J'entends pas un mot de ce que tu dis là!

Wanna take a breather?
Tu veux prendre l'air?

Drinking BOIRE

France has a long-standing love affair with wine, and as such, drinking is embedded into the culture. Kids are basically weaned on red wine, and age limits are much more lax, so they get all the crazy bingeing out of their system before they hit adulthood. People of the hipper generation still like to let loose, but drinking is a classy affair, so leave your boozy belligerence at home. You can knock a few back at a bar as normal, but equally have a glass of wine or a beer at your afternoon café sesh. The omnipresence of liquor might make it seem like there is an elevated alcohol tolerance across the nation, but really the key is in moderation. So, darling, lap up the libations but remember your *français* is gonna sound much cuter sober than slurred.

Alcohol *L'alcool*

Bartender, give me ...
M'sieu! Donnez-moi ...

> a beer.
> *une bière.*
>
> a glass of draught beer.
> *un demi.*
>
> a pint (of beer).
> *une pinte.*

a liter.
un litre.
If you're into 40s, this is your French equivalent.

some champagne.
une coupe.

a beer on tap.
une pression.

a kir.
un kir.
Kir is the French version of a wine cooler you'll see everywhere. It's cheap and good, so definitely worth a try. It's typically white wine mixed with *crème de cassis* (black currant liqueur).

a glass of (red/rosé/white) wine.
un verre du vin (rouge/rosé/blanc).

another round.
une autre tournée.

a shot of...tequila/whiskey/vodka.
un shot de...tequila/whisky/vodka.
Liquor names are essentially the same in France. Similarly, most simple cocktails are easy to figure out: *gin tonic, vodka orange, whisky coca.* Just put that *parisien* accent on it and you'll be good to go.

a corkscrew
un tire-bouchon

a bottle opener
un ouvre-bouteille/un décapsuleur

a cocktail
un cocktail

a lemon/lime
un citron/citron vert

a straw
une paille

Cheers! Here's to ...
Santé! À ...

> getting fucked up!
> *la défonce!*
>
> friendship!
> *l'amitié!*
>
> getting laid!
> *la baise!*
>
> us!
> *nous!*

I'm starting to get ...
Je commence à être ...

> tipsy.
> *pompette.*
>
> buzzed.
> *bourrée.*
>
> drunk.
> *saoul(e).*
>
> wasted.
> *fracassé(e).*
>
> really trashed!
> *complètlement défoncé(e)!*

on another planet!
complètlement à l'ouest!

sick.
malade.

I'm nauseous. I'm gonna vom.
J'ai la nausée. Je vais vomir.

Vice LE VICE

As much as the Parisian scene is about hot peeps and hot places, another couple you'll see frequently is *la clope et le cocktail* (the cig and the cocktail). Realize that the gorgeousness around you will only get hotter as you breeze past the smoke clouds. This haziness, both from inebriation and the ciggies, is what makes nightlife all the more smoldering. It might seem like a disgusting trend to us Americans but it's the gold standard in Europe, and Parisians are the kings of puffing. Weed, coke, and all the other nighttime friends might come out to play as well, but the cig reigns supreme. Sweetie, there's no use trying to escape it; that door you think is the exit will probably lead you to *le fumoir* (the smoking room). If you aren't already accustomed, get some fresh air as often as necessary and your lungs will forgive you. However, don't pick up any new habits either. Smoking may seem super sexy *à la française*, but there are a million better souvenirs you can bring back home.

Smoking *Fumer*

Pass me ...
Passe-moi ...

> a cigarette.
> *une cigarette.*

> a ciggie.
> *une clope.*

> a light.
> *du feu.*

> your pack.
> *ton paquet.*

Do you have ...? I wanna get high.
T'as ...? Je veux planer.

> a doobie
> *un pétard*

> a joint
> *un joint*

> a spliff
> *un spliff*

> some hash
> *du shit*

> some weed
> *de l'herbe*

a dealer
un dealer

Hard stuff *La drogue dure*

Yo, the guy at the bar just offered me ...
Hé, le mec au bar vient de m'offrir ...

coke.
de la coke.

a line.
une ligne.

pills.
des pillules.

X.
de l'ecsta.

Afterword ÉPILOGUE

There you have it, babe. Hopefully you now feel well equipped to talk the talk and walk the walk. Regardless if you're in Paris for one day or one year, the most important thing is to soak it up in full. It's a city to be loved and a lifestyle to be lived, so if and when you become a full-on Francophile, wear it on your sleeve, your skirt, your shoes, wherever. You should be very proud of your Parisian consecration. Opening yourself to an entirely new culture, especially the French one, is a great feat on its own, not to mention learning the language and trying to grasp the social differences. Snaps to you, girl. It might've been a little challenging, but hopefully well worth it.

So, sophisticate, what's next? Don't think that the second you leave the French borders you're suddenly back to all American. *Au contraire*, your *parisienne* persona can follow you forever. Sure you can bring a suitcase full of lovely silky, sugary gems back home, but likewise, all can appreciate your newfound way of life. Paris has a knack for inspiring people in the simplest ways: perhaps you stopped at a single flower in a garden to marvel at its beauty or sat on a bus all day to explore unknown territory; maybe you even read this entire book aloud, just to hear the melody of the language. The French like to call these intrinsic desires the *joie de vivre*. Literally translated, it means the "joy of living," but really it's so much more than that: an enthusiasm for enjoying life to the fullest. It has even been adopted into the English language, and as such it should be adopted into your life. Period. Cherish your time in Paris and hold your memories fondly. They will last a lifetime, and make your life all the lovelier.

They say, "We'll always have Paris," but now she'll always have you.

Acknowledgments

This entire experience has been my personal fairy tale, and there are countless people without whom my dream would not have come true.

To my family, specifically my parents, thank you for encouraging my lofty aspirations from an early age. Mother, you have always been my biggest enthusiast, and Dad, thank you for telling me to "follow my passion" relentlessly. Michael and Steven, I owe all my wanderlust to you.

To my friends, as my muses, you brighten my life, and I would not be the person I am today without you. Anikó, words cannot express what you mean to me, although I did try in the dedication. Jette, I am so lucky to have you as my foreign partner in crime. *Ich liebe dich*. To my Parisian posse, *merci mille fois* for taking me under your wing, being cool as f***, and teaching me everything I know.

To my colleagues at Acne Studios, thank you for all your love and support during this literary roller coaster.

To my educators, as rudimentary as it is, thank you for instructing me to read and write, well. To the French set, especially Mme. Trichard-Arany and Mme. Phillips, thank you for fueling my Francophilia.

To the publishing house of Ulysses Press, thank you for taking a chance on an unknown writer.

Lastly, to all the *Parisiennes* out there, thank you for inspiring me in the first place.

About the Author

RHIANNA JONES was born in Chicago, Illinois. Before graduating from Tufts University in 2012, with a dual-degree in International Visual Studies and French Literature, she spent her junior year abroad in Paris, fueling her affinity for French culture. Her penchant for lengthy café sittings,

photograph © Clarence de Vil

people watching, and urban exploration has followed her to New York City, where she currently lives. Combining her great passions of writing, fashion, and girliness, this book is a reminiscence of her *vie parisienne*. She is convinced of being Holly Golightly's grittier modern-day counterpart, and takes that role very seriously.